Paradoxes of Leadership

Paradoxes of Leadership

Charles R. Edmunson

with support from Loren Rodgers

Paradoxes of Leadership

Charles R. Edmunson

With support from Loren Rodgers

Cover design by Clay Stoddard

This book's production was supported by Web Industries, the National Center for Employee Ownership, and the ESOP Association.

First published 1999; reprinted 2006. Reprinted with corrections, 2009, 2012.
ISBN: 0-926902-53-9

Publisher's Note to the 2009 Reprint

This 2009 reprint of *Paradoxes of Leadership* contains substantially the same text as the original. However, it incorporates many minor edits and corrections made by Janet Edmunson, the author's widow.

This book is dedicated to
the employee-owners of Web Industries
and my wife, Janet.

Contents

About the Author

Charles Edmunson was that rare combination—a hands-on leader and a visionary. He was intimately familiar with the inner workings of both a slitting machine and the human spirit.

Until his retirement at age 49, he was the Vice President for Manufacturing at Web Industries. Web is a medium-sized employee-owned company headquartered in Westborough, Massachusetts that provides slitting services to a range of corporate clients.

At Web, Charles started as packer while in graduate school at Boston University, where he was working on a Ph.D. in Philosophy. Having lost his enthusiasm for a career in philosophy, Charles dedicated himself to working full-time at Web, where he could promote the people- and values-centered vision of Robert Fulton, the company founder.

Charles moved up to machine operator, and later department supervisor, in the Web Converting plant in Framingham, Massachusetts. When the opportunity came to open a plant in Atlanta, Charles moved there to serve as sales manager. Charles was soon promoted to plant manager, and then general manager. It was during these eight years as the senior manager of the Atlanta plant that Charles developed and tested many of the ideas in this book. During his last years in Atlanta, Charles completed his Executive MBA at Georgia State University.

In 1990, Charles was promoted to Web Industries' corporate offices in Westborough as a vice president. While he continued to practice his style of management in Westborough, he also expanded his influence to the employee stock ownership plan (ESOP) community of New England by helping to found the New England Chapter of the ESOP Association. The ESOP Association is a non-profit organization of companies with employee stock ownership plans (ESOPs).

Charles was elected president of the New England Chapter and guided that chapter to a high level of activity, serving as a model for other chapters. Charles was awarded the Outstanding Chapter Officer of the Year in 1995. His service to the national ESOP Association was also extensive, serving on two Strategic Plan Committees, the Strategic Monitoring Committee and the Board of Directors. Charles co-facilitated the meetings, which resulted in the Strategic Plan and the Vision of the ESOP Association. The ESOP Foundation created a scholarship for outstanding employee-owners in honor of Charles: the Charles R. Edmunson Scholarship. Charles spoke at events across the United States and abroad, including Hungary and China, engaging leaders everywhere in his people-centered approach to management.

Before his academic work in philosophy and his career at Web, Charles was a Minister in the Church of Christ in Jackson, Mississippi. Even though he later became an agnostic, this unique blend of spirituality and business permeated his approach to management.

Starting in May 1995, Charles developed a rare degenerative neurological disease that was later diagnosed as PSP (progressive supranuclear palsy). Over time, the disease gradually took away his ability to walk, read, talk, care for himself, and write. He died four years after this book was first published.

Charles' mission read:

*I will make a significant difference in the world by bringing grace with integrity into the lives of others. Therefore, through a disciplined focus, I will apply my life to creating **peace** for people who are in turmoil, **healing** for those who are wounded, **hope** for those in despair, and **purpose** for those who are drifting.*

Acknowledgments

I want to thank the people who have shared my work experiences with me over the last decades. Everyone at Web Industries, especially the people I know best in Atlanta and Framingham, has an important place in my heart. You, individually and as a community, helped define the trials and joys of my adult life. I especially want to thank Bob Fulton, who hired me and mentored me. Bob showed me how business can be a moral endeavor. I also want to thank Lauren Richardson for making the Tribute book, and all the people who contributed to that book.

I also want to thank Calvin Arey. We have shared more evenings, more conversations, and more insights than I can remember. Thank you for visiting me, reading to me, and helping me realize my dream of a trip to Russia. Rob Zicaro has also come by to visit me often and to talk with me about the concepts in this book.

I want to thank all the people I have come to know through the employee-ownership community. Helping the New England Chapter get off the ground and working with the Strategic Planning Committee to draft the ESOP Association's vision statement are central events in my life. I feel privileged to have shared them with such wonderful people. I especially want to thank Dick Duffy, who was my partner in both of these endeavors, June Sekera, and Steve Sheppard. I also want to thank Beth Badger, Jim Belanger, Rich Biernacki, Dean Bodem, Joe Cabral, Newt Campbell, Bill Carris, Marilyn Ceprano, Vit Eckersdorf, Dave Edgar, Rob Edwards, Ilona Eros, John Fiore, Bob Frechette, Fred Freundlich, Joel Gabrielson, Matt Guyer, Duncan Harwood, Giles Heuer, John Hoffmire, John Hover, J. Michael Keeling, Judy Kornfeld, Janos Lukacs, Chris Mackin, Don Madison, Marilyn Marchetti, Steve Marrow, Bettina McGimsey, Don Nelson, Michael Quarrey, Peter Russo, Dee Thomas, Harold Thompson, Deborah Tompkins, Richard Waddell, and Robert Withee.

There are many other people I want to thank. Dozens of people recorded books onto tape for me, which allowed me to continue thinking about leadership as well as life. Thank you to: Calvin Arey, Beth Badger,

Michael Brower, Ed Carberry, Stephen Clifford, Deborah Coffey, Rob Edwards, Gigi Fioravanti, Matt Guyer, Gail Hover, David Jacobson, Chris Mackin, Melissa McDaniels, Bettina McGimsey, Alex Moss, Dave Nadeau, Barry Pailet, Michael Quarrey, Loren Rodgers, Corey Rosen, Patty Sanford, Jayne Schmitz, Steve Schmitz, Stephen Sheppard, Ginny Vanderslice, Gary Walz, and Ryan Weeden.

I also want to thank my Georgia State University study group: Jim Burkhart, Chuck Hrushka, Gibby Kinsey, Dennis Latimer, and Kathryn Stoddard. They helped me refine my ideas on leadership, and have become some of my dearest friends.

My involvement in the planning team for Boston College's "Leadership for Change" program also influenced the ideas in this book. I would like to especially thank Steve Waddell, Charlie Derber, Joe Raelin, Sev Bruyn, Paul Gray, Bill Torbert, and Sandra Waddock.

After mentioning to my brother Ken that I wanted to write a book, he never stopped pestering me and reminding me of my intent—until I finally broke down and started writing. Thank you, Ken, for your persistence.

Many people have played central roles in making this book a reality. Corey Rosen spent at least a week editing the text. He also believed enough in me and my book to fund and spearhead the publication through the National Center for Employee Ownership. Cindy Waldron helped me write. Jill Maxwell prepared the text for publication. Kathryn Stoddard and Clay Stoddard designed and produced the cover. My brothers-in-law, Doug Mead and Jack Conlin, reviewed the text. The people who wrote their own words for this book—Steve Sheppard, Bob Fulton, Corey Rosen, Dick Duffy, Donnie Romine, June Sekera, Sid Scott, and all the people who contributed to the Tribute book—have not only my thanks, but my love.

This book would not have been possible without the help of Loren Rodgers. Loren came to our house every Sunday for over eight months. He helped me organize the stories and text. The time and effort he volunteered provided the critical contribution that helped get the book out of my head and onto paper. He deserves my sincere gratitude.

And finally, I want to thank my wife, Janet. She has been the inspiration for much of what I do and the touchstone that I need so I know that I am on the right path. Her devotion to helping me cope with the frailties of my illness is exceeded only by her generosity, humor, and steadfastness in staying with me as I confront my terminal illness. In so many ways she knows so much more than I do, and I am grateful for all she has taught me, and for the help she has given me to realize and express the things I have learned from her and from others.

When one takes a wedding vow "in sickness and in health," one is usually young and healthy. How many of us are tested on this vow, which may be easily spoken, but also easily forgotten? Janet has been tested. She is an extraordinary person who demonstrates that one human can help another reach a dream, even in the face of overwhelming difficulty. For me, this book was a dream that Janet has made possible in countless ways.

Janet: Please know that sometimes my disease is stronger than I am, and sometimes it speaks through my mouth. The disease has taken my ability to tell you, and sometimes even my ability to remember, how much I love you. It has not taken my love.

Preface

I love the title of this work. Titles are always important to me, because a title serves as the ultimate summary of whatever is said between the covers of a book. It's the triggering mechanism to help me recall what the work was about, what I derived from it, why it was something important for me to remember. In my reader's opinion, writers generally don't give enough thought to entitling their work. But Charles Edmunson has given his words careful consideration, and the title is perfect. In fact, the more I contemplated *Paradoxes of Leadership,* the more I felt drawn to the title and its implications. Let me describe to you why this title is so powerful, and why the work is, indeed, something important to remember.

First of all, *Paradoxes* is intriguing because it reflects a reality that most leaders have experienced, the existence of those happenings that seem to absolutely contradict our common-sense views of things. Let's face it: we're all drawn to those little tidbits that challenge the way that we perceive everyday reality. Out of our own experiences, or from the news, or even focused there on the cover of supermarket tabloids, we are at least curious to secretly test what we think we know. Tales of impossible survival. Scientific discovery. Aliens. Human behaviors. Like optical illusions, they tease our senses and stretch our imaginations to consider whether maybe there is another way to see the world. *Paradoxes* provides all of that intrigue by examining many of the "common sense" viewpoints about leadership that most of us have come to embrace during our work lives. For instance, how many of us would readily recognize the concept of strength through vulnerability, the subject of Charles' third paradox?

This work is powerful because it is real-life. Whether from the experiences of Charles himself, well-known leaders of history or ordinary people like you and me, *Paradoxes* is made up of the issues and questions that many of us face every day. I'm curious to know whether the contradictions and conundrums that I face are the same ones with which others struggle. I do sometimes doubt myself, the characteristic that Charles addresses in his fourth paradox. Yet somehow I seem to be comforted when I know that the issues I grapple with personally are similar to those experienced by other leaders. Like most competitive people, I find a certain satisfaction in recognizing that perhaps I have successfully dealt with an issue that tends to plague others. Also, like most business teachers/preachers I know, I am excited to gain any new insights that provide me with perspective to help others learn truths.

A second reason for the importance of this book is that it is immensely inclusive. Written works often pertain to a relatively small subset of the population—esoteric ideas that fit only a few. Yet most of us assume leadership roles somewhere in our lives, even if limited to, say, our families or immediate group of friends. The perspectives presented here are for anyone, everyone. Inclusiveness on this scale ensures that every one of us is "reading from the same page," and thus capable of identifying with each and every other reader. I think that there are few works that can make such a claim of potential connectivity.

Whenever a tool with such potential breadth of impact emerges, it is worth noting. It helps us to better recognize the struggles we have in common, as well as common solutions that may exist. It helps us to know that there are far more elements in life that make us similar than those that make us different. *Paradoxes* helps us to recognize the humanness of our leadership selves in relation to others who are traveling in the same direction. The paradoxes of leadership are universal, whether encountered within the demanding environment of my workplace or the (presumably) more relaxed activity of coaching my children's soccer teams. There is application here to an extremely wide range of my life activities. I like teachings that are so broad as to be used and reinforced throughout my day and week, and that could apply to anyone else I might meet along the way. I am validated in realizing that sometimes I, like so many others, have to get it all wrong before I can get it right, the focus of paradox 13.

My third reason for admiring these thoughts and experiences is that this entire work constitutes several paradoxes itself. In addition to the ironies and seeming contradictions contained in the words themselves, the structure, content, and history of this book all combine to create an extraordinarily moving and paradoxical story of its own.

At fewer than one hundred pages in length, *Paradoxes* may be one of the shortest books I have ever read on the massive subject of leadership. Yet the pages contain more introspective instruction and depth than volumes ten times as large. Perhaps Charles has practiced what he preaches in paradox 6, in which he suggests that less really is more. But that which has been left unsaid has definitely not been ignored. Rather, the unstated has been left for each of us to complete. In the most subtle of ways, Charles has demonstrated his first paradox about having more influence in listening than in telling. I found myself responding out loud to Charles as I read *Paradoxes,* knowing that he would be listening to my self-instruction, of course.

This topic of leadership may be the most written about, dissected, analyzed, debated, studied subject in the whole of Western society. We discuss the leadership characteristics of people ranging from Jesus to Machiavelli, from Gandhi to MacArthur. In the process, the true leadership traits of these historical figures sometimes become obscured by their other personality traits. The idea of what constitutes effective leadership can become clouded in the mixture. Leadership becomes a very complex issue as a result, as we "students" often resort to simply emulating the personalities and behaviors of these figures. Alternatively, *Paradoxes* drives us inward to seek our own leadership solutions based upon who we are.

Paradoxes helps to direct us. It does so, not by blueprinting or boilerplating, but by positing fourteen observations that we, in turn, must consider and internalize for ourselves. Essentially we become the historical figures under scrutiny as we try to identify our very own unique, leadership strengths. Charles has held out the possibility, the likelihood, that the secret to effective leadership lies within us if we will be introspective enough to discern it. Rather than an immensely complicated field, the topic of leadership in *Paradoxes* is reduced to personal proportions.

As a result of the above-mentioned qualities, the book serves as a learning tool that puts the real burden of teaching onto the student/reader. It seems an ingenious methodology to me, because it bears out another long-standing paradox of life that says that in order to truly learn a subject, I must teach it. Charles did not cite that one in his work, but it is clearly implied by the very approach he has taken to helping us in our learning quests.

Amidst all of these paradoxes within *Paradoxes,* there is one that is the most instructive and moving of all. It is the power of these words delivered by a man who cannot speak. After a lifetime of articulating his own inner beliefs about leadership, and demonstrating through his actions the truth of those beliefs, Charles Edmunson cannot speak now due to an illness that has no recognizable name, no respite and no cure. Charles is now immobilized, as well, the bonds of a wheelchair now restraining the energies of a man who ran for 1,400 days in a row until he was no longer able to rise from that chair. The sheer physical process of committing his values, philosophies, and fervently held beliefs to writing serves as an act of courage and leadership by itself. It is a rare circumstance, indeed, that this book can deliver learning from the author, from the reader, and from the sheer presence of the volume itself, as a tangible evidence of the paradoxes of leadership. Ultimately, that is why I love the title and the importance of what it represents.

If *Paradoxes of Leadership* helps even one reader to understand, accept, and improve leadership effectiveness, it will be a leadership lesson of the highest order, given from the perspective of a full life, and from the heart of Charles' Final Paradox: A Full Life Is Achieved Not By Grasping, But By Giving. Charles has given us a gift for the new millennium, and beyond . . . .

Stephen C. Sheppard
Northfield, Minnesota
November 1998

Introduction

It's a five o'clock world
when the whistle blows
no one owns a piece of my time.

—Allen Reynolds, 1965

(from the song "Five O'Clock World," performed by The Vogues)

In our corporate office, there is a smoking room where all the smokers go to get their cigarettes. The smokers tend to get close to one another, spending their lunches together and building their own culture, talking frankly about their own situations. The Coke machines are also there, and I'm addicted to Diet Coke. When I went to the vending machines one time, I overheard a woman saying, "My self-esteem is being tortured in this job because I'm not using my potential."

I do not remember what she looked like. I do not remember her face or how her voice sounded. I would not recognize her in the smoking room today. But her phrase—"my self-esteem is being tortured"—echoes through my mind like the motto of a generation. Partly because I do not know her or the details of her situation, she has become almost an archetype to me.

Too many people are selling their lives away for a paycheck. This woman is one more example. There are people like her in the company where you work.

~

Why should a business leader care about the quality of work life? Some will say that the business of business is business. People are selling their lives for a paycheck, but maybe it is a fair deal. They choose to do it every day, after all. Even if employees are alienated from their work, the money they earn still lets them live the life they want to after working hours.

You should care about alienation in your workforce for one simple bottom-line business reason: An alienated work force is a half-engaged work force.

Alienation can be "classic"—like someone repeatedly pounding a series of rivets. Alienation can also be more modern—someone who is mindlessly following invoicing procedures they know they could improve on. Alienation can also be more subtle: Imagine someone who cares passionately about her job, but has no interest in how it fits into the company as a whole. Or someone who does good work, but cares about his job evaluations more than customer satisfaction.

These people are not using their full self at work. To some extent, they have all left their brains at the door, or at least part of their brains. Alienation is another way of saying that a person's potential is being under-used. And your company cannot afford that anymore. Alienation is now too high a price to pay. It is what keeps you from getting more out of your human resources.

Alienation on the job is the relic of a previous time, a time when the only way to coordinate a large group of people in a single task was to fix each person's role in the task and then fit the whole system together like a puzzle. Pieces could not change in the middle of the task, because one piece would no longer fit with the others. The strength of this system is that one cog does not need to know what is happening with another cog. They are independent. Changes in the market are processed at the top and dictated to the bottom. This rigid system worked like magic, coordinating people into rational organizations, efficiently producing the goods that fueled the American century, winning a world war and building a commercial empire.

Technology played a crucial role in building our modern world and our modern corporations, but no one interested in business should forget that one of the most important innovations of the last two centuries is not technical, but an "engineering" style of management. Theodore Levitt writes:

> The real significance of the nineteenth century is not the Industrial Revolution, with its shift from animal to machine power, but the managerial revolution, with its shift from the craftsman's functional independence to the manager's rational routines.

The nineteenth-century principle of rational management was perfected in the twentieth century. Efficiency experts helped companies divide tasks into the smallest replicable units possible, then measured how quickly each person did his task. The goal was to eliminate the mental input of the worker into the job. Instead, a limited number of professionals and managers was charged with any responsibilities to design, create, innovate, and change.

These last paragraphs may feel out of date and irrelevant to you and your company. The images are of lumbering factories. Your organization may not share much at all with these factories of yore. The machines, if there are any, are newer, safer, and quieter. The work day is shorter. Pay is higher. Your Information Technology (IT) may be top rate and actively used by all employees in their day-to-day work. The closest thing to child labor is a college internship. The mindset of the Industrial Revolution may seem distant and irrelevant.

But the management style of the nineteenth century is with us still. When technology changed from steam-driven to electric and internal combustion motors in the nineteenth century, it took decades for people to adapt systems to exploit the new opportunities these machines created. Even architecture took decades to move from the multi-storied approach that could best use steam-driven motors to the assembly-line approach electricity allowed. In the twentieth century, it has taken decades to use computers as more than fast adding machines. If architecture and machine function take decades to catch up to technology, imagine how difficult it is for attitudes to catch up to the new conditions.

Many managerial reflexes, reflexes that feel inherent and natural, are holdovers from the old revolution. The principles of nineteenth-century rational management are taught in the operations management classes at business schools, or they were until recently enough that they are hardwired into the structures of our companies. These principles live on, slightly modified but fundamentally unchanged, in the management culture of America.

～

There are more books on the massive changes in the business world than a single person can read. Here, I just want to focus on two of the features of the new business environment that help frame the basic subject of this book.

1. *Information technology has grown up.* In previous decades the only way to coordinate a large number of people toward a single goal was to give them carefully designed and fixed roles. This is no longer true. Organizations can share information precisely and quickly enough to allow each employee to adjust her actions to the changing demands of the day. We have the ability to move beyond rigidly engineered structures.

2. *Globalization.* With the full maturity of an ever-increasing number of countries, and the blossoming of world trade, each individual producer is under mounting pressure to create the most value from each expense dollar. Companies from an ever-expanding number of countries are entering markets with low-price, high-quality products. So businesses are getting squeezed in two directions at the same time: more customer delight—quality, turnaround, customization—for fewer dollars.

Logically speaking, your company needs more revenue per dollar of expense. And that includes labor dollars.

Corporate America has tried downsizing. It has succeeded in some cases and failed in others. But downsizing is an inherently limited solution: Eventually you run out of employees to remove from your payroll. The real solution is a company full of workers who think and have the tools to act independently in the best interests of the company. Companies now have to make more decisions about more things more quickly. They need ideas and information from their work forces and often need workers to be able to make decisions on their own or in groups.

I am referring to something different from Total Quality Management (TQM), empowerment, or quality circles. These programs can be wonderful. They provide step-by-step guidelines about what can work and what probably will not. But lists of procedures and recipes, no matter how carefully researched or how exact their implementation, are insufficient. These solutions represent a variant of the engineering approach to human resources. People are still viewed as inputs, as factors of production. The underlying assumption can be stated as, "Machines need maintenance, and people do as well. It's just that their maintenance is a bit more complicated." These management ideas can be merely maintenance for people, to keep them well-oiled parts of the corporate machine.

At the risk of stating the obvious, people are more than machines. They are qualitatively different. I want to talk about two differences.

First, machines are inherently limited—they cannot do more than their design permits. People are potentially unlimited. Their capacity for growth and self-improvement means that, given a nurturing environment, their potential contribution to the company is infinite.

The other difference, which is a core assumption of this book, is that people are emotional beings before they are rational beings. People have expectations, hopes, and fears. Machines do not. People assess you at the same time you assess them. They try to guess what you think of them, and what you think they think. Machines do none of this. People are constantly reading each other, whether they do it consciously or subconsciously. To manage people, it is not enough to have the right answers. You need to relate to the people you manage in a way that develops their ability and their desire to find the right answers on their own. You need to say the right things with your words, and you need to send off the right cues and body language so that they believe your words.

Fundamentally, management is about human interaction, about learning to communicate with people in a way that encourages everyone to engage his fullest capacities. Management demands strength of character and depth of commitment. Human beings are inherently complex, and interactions between people are even more complex. Personalities are nuanced and multilayered; what works well as a management approach to one person may fail with another.

I believe that the single largest barrier to unlocking the profit-making human potential of our work forces is leadership. I mean leadership in a very broad sense: I include honesty, vision, grace, patience, and humility. Some of these characteristics have very little to do with what we commonly conceive of as the concern of a business leader. In this book I will share very personal principles, some of which may feel as if they have nothing to do with your role as a manager.

You may be thinking that you are no longer interested in reading this book. You may already focus on these issues. If so, then you are doing well. You are managing better than most, and I congratulate you. But, still, there is always room for growth. Are you amazed by the skills, dedication, and creativity of everyone in your company? Are you caught off guard by people coming up with solutions before problems arise? Or before the problem occurs to you?

Perhaps you feel you need concrete suggestions, not moralizing homilies about character and grace. Let me put one challenge to you. If you accept my premise that the future of business lies in engaging a wider range of our workforce's talents, then it seems logical that businesses need to encourage the human fulfillment of their employees. Here is my challenge: Tell me a way that human potential can be fulfilled in a company without management leading the way. I am convinced that managers must not only be struggling as individuals with their own personal fulfillment, but that they also must go beyond that and be mentors to other people. They must understand something about human vulnerability and growth so that they can help the people who report to them to grow and develop. And since this is necessarily an introspective, personal process, company leaders can no longer shy away from interacting with their work forces as one human to another. No book will be a foolproof path to fulfillment or leadership. Here, I want to share some of the things I have learned in my tenure as a manager.

The nineteenth-century revolution to rational management has run its course. We need a twenty-first-century revolution: a revolution to nurturing management.

~

Fyodor Dostoevsky, the great Russian novelist, said in his book The House of the Dead *that to utterly crush the spirit of a man, just give him work of a completely senseless, irrational nature. Kristine, a worker in our Framingham plant, was heading toward being a character out of Dostoevsky's works. She said she just followed the boss' orders; that there was no creativity in her job. Given the opportunity, however, she grasped the chance. Her supervisor saw the passion in her eyes and helped her move from being a packer to a machine operator over a three-year period. She received an award from the company for her exemplary work. She has hope for the future. My father used to say that "too many people quit looking for work when they find a job." Kristine had done that until someone put faith in her.*

It is not enough to advance in the workplace, or even to do an exemplary job. People want to feel that they matter, that they are making a contribution to those around them. A machine operator in one of our plants once told me with great emotion that he did not want to end up just wasting his life. The feeling in his voice when he said that has stayed with me ever since. Over the years, he became a team leader, one of our best, because he evokes the best in the people he leads. He makes a difference.

We were once in need of another customer service person. We advertised in the newspaper and received a number of replies. I picked out three or four of the most promising to start interviewing. I took one applicant to the shop floor where people were making things. I could see her excitement mounting as she talked with several groups of people. "I've never seen anything like this," she said. "The last place I worked, I could tell who had been there for more than two years: Their eyes were dead."

THE FOURTEEN PARADOXES

Paradox 1
We have more influence when we listen than when we tell

Paradox 2
Profound change comes from a feeling of safety, not from fear

Paradox 3
We are stronger when we are vulnerable

Paradox 4
Even when we are effective, we doubt ourselves

Paradox 5
Our strength is our weakness

Paradox 6
Less is more

Paradox 7
Our strength comes through serving, not through dominating

Paradox 8
We correct better through grace than through confrontation

Paradox 9
We gain respect not by demanding it, but by giving it

Paradox 10
We learn by talking, not just by listening

Paradox 11
With people, the shortest distance between two points is not a straight line

Paradox 12
The hard stuff is the soft stuff

Paradox 13
Sometimes we have to get it wrong to get it right

The Final Paradox:
A full life is achieved not by grasping but by giving

Paradox 1

WE HAVE MORE INFLUENCE WHEN WE LISTEN THAN WHEN WE TELL.

If a manager's job is to give direction to a group of people, then the most obvious way for a manager to do his job is to tell people what to do. That minimizes ambiguity and maximizes the chances that everyone will coordinate. Everyone depends on the manager to provide direction.

But this approach is also extravagantly wasteful, and leaders who breed dependence are not effective. If people always look to a manager for direction, then they are not very likely to turn around and suggest the new ways of looking at or doing things that can really move the company forward.

There are several ways you can breed dependence. If you second-guess people, people will stop venturing their ideas. If you assert your opinions more strongly than anyone else, people will be intimidated from sharing what they think. If you ask people what they think, but only because you know that "participative managers" are supposed to do that, people will say things only to make you happy. If you insist on approving every decision, people will stop making suggestions.

Effective leaders, by contrast, really listen. They know that listening to employees provides direction more effectively than telling employees what to do. Without someone to listen, employees have no reason to develop their ideas. And if employees are not actively thinking about the company, they are already half-engaged. Leaders can engage people to the point where the company becomes an idea factory, where people want to share their knowledge because they know it will be considered and, when it makes sense, used.

Chuck Colson and Jack Eckerd write in *Why America Doesn't Work* that "sometimes management seems blind to the message it sends to workers." Managers focus on profits, but workers focus more on the meaning of their work. Profits matter, of course. Profits are what allow companies to do the things that make work meaningful. But providing meaning to people's jobs can also create profits. If people are fully engaged, the company will make more money. If a boss just tells people what to do, people just work to collect a paycheck. Your company needs more than that.

Karl Marx talked about alienation from work, meaning that people derived no meaning from their jobs. When people owned their own tools of production—the farmer, the guild member, the artisan—meaning was plain to see. Their work was their own, it reflected their own ideas and skills. And it fed their families. But with the rise of the industrial state, workers became time sellers, selling their days to those who now owned the factories. Employee ownership is part of the way we at Web Industries and thousands of other companies help address this problem. Now people work for themselves. Employee ownership is not enough, however. People also need to feel invested emotionally in their jobs. You accomplish this by listening, by giving people a way to share their interest in the company, to contribute their insights, and to have their ideas taken seriously. People can see they make a difference in how the company does business. Is there any business that would not do better if it could capture the good ideas of all its workers, and not just its managers?

Listening Well

Listening cannot be just a mechanical device. Leaders cannot just say that from 3 o'clock to 4 o'clock on Friday they will open their office doors and listen to people's ideas. They cannot listen and then do whatever they had been planning from the start. They cannot just listen to words either. Leaders need to learn to read faces, to hear emotions. People are emotional beings before they are rational beings. We react emotionally first and only think through things enough to react rationally later. If you spend the effort to look at people's faces, you can listen to their hearts. That can make all the difference in knowing whether people perceive your efforts as genuine. You will see whether they are telling you what they think or what they think you want them to say.

To get this process started, it is important to ask questions. People are not just going to pipe up to management on their own initiative, at least not very often. We have all been trained to think of the boss as, well, the boss. They want us to do, not think; to listen, not speak. So to get people to share what they know, you need to learn to ask. Just saying "What do you think?" may not be enough, however. You need to practice the art of probing, asking people specific questions that require them to give considered responses.

Building a consensus that this is the way management really works will take a lot of time, but perhaps not as much as you think. Once you reach a critical momentum, the process will build on itself. People will gain trust in you. And this is where the paradox really plays out. Managers who succeed in engaging people become the focal point for a cascade of ideas and information. The training, experience, and innate capacity that got them to the management level can now be used to help sift through these ideas to discern which ones will help the company. No matter how good you are at generating ideas on your own, it is most unlikely you could generate as many good ideas as you can by listening.

But the process only starts here. When people learn to trust you, and you learn to trust them, you can turn over more decision making to them. Within mutually acceptable guidelines, they do not even need to tell you their ideas anymore; they can just act. Now you have the time to engage your own skills at a higher level of abstraction, and you can ask the same of more of the people with whom you work. When everyone starts to listen, everyone becomes an idea sifter and processor. Your company becomes, in Peter Senge's phrase, "a learning company."

~

I was proud of my knowledge of our machines. I had been a machine operator myself, so I felt that I had a powerful combination of hands-on experience and theoretical perspective. During my very first managerial experience, we received an expedited order. To make sure things got done, I told one of our operators how he should run the job. But he lived and breathed with this machine every day. By casting aside his opinions, the worst outcome happened. He rebelled against me and ran the machine just the opposite of the way I told him to—and that was not even the way he thought it should be done. He never confronted me; he just did it. We never did get his insights into how the machine should really be run. He ended up leaving the company not long after that.

It took a few more incidents like this before I figured out that maybe people know how to run their machines better than I do.

~

But what if the ideas people contribute are bad ideas? Whenever I hear someone use the phrase "bad idea," it tells me something about them. A particular idea may not be a good one in the sense of being a rational option for the company. But the very fact that people are contributing ideas is a good sign, a sign that they are engaged and will come up with something useful eventually, especially if they are helped to understand why this particular idea would not work. "Bad ideas" need to be encouraged, even celebrated. People need to feel good about their bad ideas if they are to keep contributing. Leaders need to help people see, however, how to generate better ideas, how to think through the processes at hand so that the bad idea becomes a learning experience that will help improve the next idea. We need to help people learn from the problems in their ideas by asking them hard questions gently posed, questions that can help them think through the issues.

It is also important to recognize that listening is not just one-on-one. Managers need to encourage employees to talk about ideas among themselves and listen to each other, a process that can help them refine ideas into good proposals. This exchange may be through formal participation in work groups or informally on the floor. When people share ideas and information between themselves, they create synergy. All of us have had the experience of hearing someone say something that triggers an idea, or of suggesting something and someone else being able to add to it. This process demonstrates that none of us is as smart as all of us.

In the end, of course, there will be ideas that just will not work. Managers are managers because they have to be able to say no in these situations, but "no" should be the last resort, not the first reaction.

∼

I know of a manager at one of the companies I came into contact with through the ESOP community. He had graduated from an elite business school, and his forte was not listening—it was thinking. People always shut down around him because they saw he thought his perspective was always right. They could not relate to him. They thought he was arrogant and did not see their ideas as valuable. He recognized some ideas as worthwhile, but not many—and he quickly took personal ownership of those ideas he did like. People started keeping their ideas to themselves for fear of looking like fools. The factory started losing money.

I decided he needed some mentoring, and encouraged a friend at his company to speak with him on a weekly basis. He has learned a lot over the last several years about how to nurture people's ideas. He is more emotionally literate than before. He did not read people's faces when he started with the company, but he has made real progress now.

Paradox 2

PROFOUND CHANGE COMES FROM A FEELING OF SAFETY, NOT FROM FEAR.

An old African proverb says that one who has been bitten by a snake will be afraid of anything that wiggles. Fear, the proverb tells us, is a learned trait. Fear in the work place is similarly conditioned. Like fear of wiggly things, it can also be overcome. Leaders do this by creating a safe environment for people. To many people, leadership means being able to tell people what to do, even to inspire fear in people. That is not leadership; it is control. Real leadership comes not from intimidation, but from creating safety.

Those in management often think that by chastising people for errors, they will see where they have gone wrong and change. The assumption is that people, acting rationally, will disengage the message from its emotional content. But people often listen through the filter of their fears. They may or may not learn about the particular issue at hand, but they will learn, in the emotional sense, not to trust the manager, to fear for their job security, and to worry about their loss of status.

～

One secretary did a superb job with our company. She told me how horrible her past job was compared to Web. A couple of days after that, she found a card on her desk. She immediately reverted to her fear mode. It took her hours to open the card, which, when she did, was pink. She told me she was sure she was being fired. It was, in fact, a positive message from her boss, but she was almost in tears.

～

When people feel safe at work, they will be more comfortable with taking the risks required to share their ideas and information. Think of the risks involved. Will I appear foolish? Will the boss "just say no"? Will I be chastised for wasting my time? Will my colleagues think I am raising the bar for them, or just trying to apple polish? Will someone else take credit for my idea anyway? Unless we create a feeling of safety, one that fosters the sense that even mistakes are OK if they are made in the spirit of trying to move the company forward, we will not succeed in engaging people.

Creating a safe environment does not mean that you should paste a permanent smile on your face. Everyone knows that leaders have to deal with unpleasant situations—wearing a plastic expression at those times makes people wonder about your sincerity. And of course, there are times when leaders will, and should, get angry. It is important, however, to think about this anger and the impact it will have. Are you getting angry because nothing else can get people's attention? (I did this once at our Atlanta plant when people were not keeping the bathrooms clean in our new building.) Are you getting angry because people are violating basic rules of conduct in the company? Anger might be justified in these situations. But even anger needs to be followed by grace, by an acknowledgment that, the present problem aside, you assume the best in people. In the end, as Samuel Smiles has said, "The only relationships in the world that have ever been worthwhile and enduring have been those in which one person could trust another."

Paradox 3

WE ARE STRONGER WHEN WE ARE VULNERABLE.

Arrogance and vulnerability can be seen as opposites. Arrogant management assumes it always knows what is best. To make sure people get the message, arrogant managers will make decisions even about things they do not know much about. The result, of course, is not just bad decisions, but a lot of angry workers who lose whatever faith they had in management. By contrast, a willingness to be vulnerable, to say "I don't know the best way to do this" can build trust among employees, a feeling that management knows what it can do and what it must rely on others to do. Paradoxically, managers become more respected and more effective when they can admit vulnerability than when they insist they know everything.

When leaders insist on doing things a certain way and refuse to admit that they might be wrong, they are weaker, not stronger. One time in Atlanta, I insisted a machine could do a job it actually could not do. A customer needed a product slit to a narrow width, and I promised we could fill the order. It turned out we could not do it. I had to call the customer to apologize, but we never heard from that customer again. People were afraid of me because I was "the expert." They withheld their own knowledge and experience from me. My own arrogance kept me from admitting I did not know—in fact, it led me to intimidate people into thinking I did. If I had exposed my vulnerability, people might have opened up and told me what the machines could and could not do—and we might still have that customer.

What would have happened to my leadership, however, had I admitted I was not an expert? Think about how you have reacted to bosses who claimed to know everything. Did you think they were really as smart as they said they were, or did you just see them as arrogant? Think even of personal relationships. We often think the people who are the smartest are those who, rather than claiming to know all the answers, instead consistently ask the most interesting, intriguing, and probing questions. We often like the people best whose questioning shows an interest in us.

The "know-it-alls" do not get our respect, much less our followership. The people who ask us nothing about ourselves are people we would rather not see again.

Effective leaders ask insightful questions. Unlike the people they are asking, leaders are in the unique position of being able to gather information from all sources. They spend their time evaluating the larger picture for their operational unit. This does not make them an expert in any particular facet of the operation—the people doing the work usually are more expert—but it makes them the expert in knowing what questions to ask and how to integrate insights from across the company. Leaders who show an interest in people's ideas also generate more ideas from those people. That added information enhances the leader's strengths.

A corollary of this paradox is that sharing company-wide vulnerabilities—bad news—can be a strength as well. Lots of companies fall into the trap of focusing on the good news, fearing people will get demoralized if they hear a lot of bad news. Of course, troubles are never completely hidden. People know something is wrong; they just do not know the details. Often, the truth is not as bad as the stories running through the rumor mill and people's imaginations. Hearing the real dimensions of a problem can reassure people that it is something they can overcome. Sharing bad news also lets people start to deal with the source of the problem. It gives them the chance to move away from passive hopelessness and into a roll-up-their-sleeves-and-do-something position. Finally, it gives credibility to all the good news you share.

When bad news is shared, the first thing to do is state the condition as clearly as possible. Then you want to brainstorm as many ideas as possible. Do not criticize people's ideas at this point; it only discourages people from creative thinking. It could be that an unorthodox solution is needed, one that people would be reluctant to propose if they thought it would be subject to a critique right away. Often, the right answers will become obvious, and there will be no need ever to critique ideas. More often, though, once all the ideas are on the table, you can pick out the most interesting ones and start to meld, dissect, and change them into a workable approach. All those other ideas that do not make it into this process are simply discarded, not attacked.

Paradox 4

EVEN WHEN WE ARE EFFECTIVE, WE DOUBT OURSELVES.

We have been planning meetings at our company every quarter that involve all general managers from across the company. At these meetings, because we are an employee-owned company, we focus on financial issues and general issues brought forth by the managers. We try to design these meetings so that the participants feel heard and acknowledged.

One of our managers doubted himself a lot. It showed in his apparent arrogance, a way we often hide our doubts. He tended to be critical in our meetings, often throwing a monkey wrench into what we were trying to do. He asked hostile questions and grimaced at other people's remarks. Other people were reluctant to participate because of his stance. In thinking about how to deal with this person, I thought the best approach might be to ask him to lead the meeting, to take responsibility for producing something positive. He was reluctant initially, but eventually agreed. He ended up doing a very good job, bringing some new perspectives, particularly about the company's culture. As a result of his efforts, subsequent meetings became more participative and interactive, whereas before they had consisted mostly of a series of reports.

Interestingly, he had never previously raised his concerns about our meeting structure. He tried to ask some questions, but was reluctant to seem to dominate. After the meeting, people praised his good work, but he told me he thought it had been a mistake for him to take the lead. He was not convinced he had really added anything, even with all the positive feedback he got. He still doubted himself.

Even as great a leader as Thomas Jefferson suffered self-doubts. Jefferson founded the University of Virginia, a school that was to embody Jefferson's democratic leanings by getting people more involved in their own education rather than just following the dictates of a board of regents. Jefferson saw the University as his greatest contribution to the world. But I heard a story about Jefferson that affected me deeply. Shortly after the founding of the University, a student riot occurred. I have read that Jefferson, on stage in public, sobbed, "My whole life has been a failure."

While none of us wants to live a life of self-doubt, and while too much doubt will paralyze us from taking any action, an element of self-doubt may actually help us to lead. For one thing, it makes it easier for others to connect with us. The leader who always seems totally in command may also seem remote and unapproachable. Self-doubt also keeps us questioning our own actions and motives, searching for a better way to do things. Finding the right balance (and it will be different for everyone) between confidence and doubt is one of the critical tasks of becoming a leader.

Paradox 5

OUR STRENGTH IS OUR WEAKNESS.

"It is lonely at the top." How many times have you heard that about leaders? There are many common reasons for leaders to feel alone. Subordinates can become sycophants. People may not tell you what they think, but what they think you want them to say. People may start to relate to you in your role rather than to you as a person. Think of the way you may have reacted to a CEO or political official whose authority you respected. Were their jokes a little funnier? Their observations a little more insightful? Were you really reacting to them the way you would an ordinary colleague, or were you reacting to the position they had?

This reaction is natural. Leaders have power, which they can use to help or hinder the careers of people they supervise. People may be reluctant not just to criticize leaders, but even to praise them, fearing they will look like apple polishers. Social relationships between people of unequal power in a company can be problematic. Leaders may fear that a social relationship with a colleague may lead to charges of favoritism by other employees. Employees may assume that "the boss" would not want to socialize with people who are not "peers."

It is generally accepted that strength breeds isolation—but it is rarely recognized that this isolation is itself a weakness. Most serious is the way it results in distorted information. In a sort of corporate perversion of "if you don't have anything nice to say, don't say anything at all," people say what they think leaders want to hear, or do not tell them anything. The more layers between a leader and employees, the worse this dysfunction becomes. Effective leaders need to recognize this weakness and seek methods to circumvent it. By working hard to build trust, they find ways that people can be comfortable in being frank with them. A good leader should, in Edward Deming's phrase, drive out fear.

There is more to this than just being an effective manager. Leaders are people too, and need relationships to balance their lives. No human being is complete in himself or herself. Even if you have family and friends outside of the company, work is too important a part of our lives to ignore relationships within it.

At Web, I tried to deal with this issue by partnering with a close colleague. Each month, I had an off-site meeting with a partner—Dan. Dan was someone I trusted. We could talk at length and frankly. His perspective enriched mine; I hope my views helped him. While this was a structured program, I also tried to expose my vulnerabilities by being emotionally available to people, showing that I was Charles, not just a position with a management title. It was something that needed conscious work every day.

> I just finished a year of being a leader on the second shift at our plant. I could not always tell if I was effective. You try to look for change in others; if you see change, it validates your feelings of accomplishment. Sometimes, though, it is hard to tell if there really is change. I would ask myself, did I make the change happen, or was it the environment? For me, a central way of dealing with this is by enlisting the aid of a "coach" or mentor. I had such a coach during my studies at school. My coach served as a "third eye." Coaches can provide you with a different perspective. They see things you cannot. It may be best to form a partnership with someone who is most unlike you. This keeps you from "feel good" clone thinking. Groups often form around people with similar views. If you are a mentor, this can lead to dangerous forms of group think. Getting people with different views to provide feedback is a way out of this loop.
>
> —*Rob Zicaro, Web Employee*

Leaders who take on the traditional model of strength—"I know best, follow me up the hill"—fail to encourage independent thought. Real leaders know they do not know everything. They engage their people in helping to solve problems. Involving people means admitting our limitations and weaknesses. The other possibility, pretending that we have no weaknesses, is itself a weakness. It is arrogance.

How do we know if we are arrogant? We have to have self-insight, and we need partners who can point out that we are being perceived as arrogant. I talked earlier about my partner, Dan. I trust him deeply. You must take risks to develop a partner who will be frank with you. We all need someone who will say bluntly what we need to hear, and who will say it with compassion and grace.

Paradox 6

LESS IS MORE.

Leaders are very busy. The more people they have working for them the less time they have. But leaders need to choose how to use their time. A leader is commissioned to lead people to achieve the best possible group effort, not to churn out the work herself. A leaders' most efficient use of time is bringing out the best in other people—not being expert in everything and much less trying to do everything. Instead, effective leaders help their followers do the best work possible by listening to them, encouraging them, and touching base with them every day.

We have all known leaders—perhaps you are one of them—who say "I *could* teach people to do this, but they wouldn't be able to do it as fast or as well. I'm rushed now, so it's easier just to do it myself." These leaders may be heroic in their efforts and even their competency, but they are not building organizational strength and, eventually, they will burn out. Leaders need to drop some of their tasks in favor of nurturing people who can carry out tasks for them.

It is a truism that leaders need to delegate responsibility, but delegation is not enough. Leaders need to impart energy to people so that they want to take on the tasks. The job of a leader in this respect is not just being a cheerleader, however. The skilled leader knows who should have what degree of autonomy in making decisions. Leaders need to know what training, encouragement, information, and help from other people can move someone from being overwhelmed by an obligation to being challenged by it. Leaders need to know when to delegate to an individual and when to call on a team.

There are no simple guidelines for how to do this; much is instinctive, but most is just making the effort, being open to learning from your mistakes, and looking to find ways to help people take on more responsibility. I have learned some principles, however, that might help you in this process. Ask first who can guide this project with a minimum amount of coaching. Who else can learn this project and maybe take it over? Identify the people who can help you. If there is something that needs to be done right away, maybe you should have the person accompany you, and watch how you do it—but think about what kind of training you can provide to people so they can take over the next time. If one person does not have the skills, maybe a combination of people would, or could learn them if given the proper resources. It is always tempting to say "I could just do this myself faster or better," but in the long run, by growing the talents of people around you, you build an organization that can do a lot more things than you could ever do on your own.

But how do you nurture someone? You nurture by giving them time, attention, and projects that are not too hard and not too easy. Support them by meeting with them regularly. Review the projects for which they are responsible. Listen to them. Explore their learning. Make sure they understand the importance of their project. Give them public recognition for their achievements. Counsel them through their frustrations. Maybe they will fail—if the project fails and the person learned a lot through the project, admire the learning and do not dwell on the failure. If people turn out to lack the interest or the ability to do a job well, keep nurturing them. Maybe they do not have the talents for the particular tasks you had assigned to them. Everyone can do something, so work on finding something else.

"Can you nurture everyone you supervise?" I think so. Everyone can be nurtured to handle some things they have never handled before. You cannot, of course, nurture everyone at once. The ultimate challenge of leadership is to teach people to nurture others. A healthy organization is one where people nurture others to be their better selves. The people you nurture can in turn nurture others. It is a positive feedback loop and illustrates one of the most powerful ways in which less really can be more.

Devoting Time to People

Clearly, one of the essential elements of this paradox is that leaders have to spend a lot of time with people getting them to do the things the leader might (correctly or incorrectly) feel he could more easily do himself. The time you spend with people is the manifestation of your commitment to people, and people see it in ways you cannot anticipate.

Spending time with the people you manage is like exercise—if you are not really committed you will always find an excuse not to do it. My wife has an off-site meeting with her employees once a month and meets with her direct reports once a week. The meetings build a context for everyone's daily work. There was danger of her department going out of existence due to her company's financial pressures, but her efforts created a strong, effective team that has thrived in the face of numerous downsizings.

I used to work for a manager who was too busy to help me with anything. He was not a partner to me but a boss. I did not feel like I could ask him anything. He gave me no energy. He was very busy himself. When I got through to him finally, I talked to him about this and he explained that he just had too much to do. Instead of valuing me, he valued the time to do projects himself. I was just a means of getting another project done. He did not pay attention to me because of his own priorities: to get his job done, not the organization's job. The more he focused on his own work, the less he and I collectively, accomplished.

Paradox 7

OUR STRENGTH COMES THROUGH SERVING, NOT THROUGH DOMINATING.

"Servant leadership" has become a catchword in management circles lately. Lots of managers like to describe their organizations as "inverted pyramids" where management's purpose is to make life easier for all the people who work with them. Like most management nostrums, this is one that is verbalized more than practiced. In fact, managers tend to dominate most of the time. At one plant that we toured, everyone saluted the manager in charge!

The need to be dominant is not surprising. Whatever the official corporate rhetoric, management gets ahead in most cases by being able to say "I did that." Being able to dominate is, for many people, a basic means of self-affirmation. People often need to take credit, not give it; to direct, rather than take orders. There is something more subtle going on as well, however. For at least some employees, it is easier to have a dominant boss. Then employees do not have to take responsibility themselves, whether for learning or for doing. The domineering boss becomes a force for social cohesion among employees, and some employees can assume social leadership roles by being the ones to lead the carping about the boss. A domineering boss also drives out ambiguity at work. People know what they are expected to do; they can do it and go home at night and forget about work.

In other words, the domineering boss is not just an artifact of an obsolete management system, but also an expression of some basic personal and social needs. At the same time, however, managerial domination deeply violates other needs and, as I have argued, is dysfunctional for the company. A servant leader, one who works to help others build their abilities and responsibilities, and who strives to make other people's jobs easier, creates a more challenging workplace. People have an opportunity to grow and, as a result, contribute much more to the company. Servant leadership requires a strength of character in managers that is not all that common. Done well, however, it can help create, in journalist John Case's words, a "company of business people."

When I was managing the Atlanta plant for my company, the work came in spurts. We were growing faster than we could increase production. Because the primary problem we faced was a shortage of person-power, I would come in to help people unpack and run the machines on Saturdays. Because it was not normal work time, there were no management issues at stake. I would end up spending a lot of time at work in those days. It was worth it, however, because in doing this manufacturing work, I gained the respect of the people in the plant.

> In order to practice servant leadership, you have to be genuine. You cannot fake it. It is not a technique, it is a reflection of your belief in people. People are not stupid: They'll see through it. It is out of context and people will know that. You may use some techniques as a servant leader, but that is not what servant leadership is.
>
> One danger of servant leadership, however, is anarchy—leaders so eager to turn over responsibility that no one knows who is in charge of what. We discovered that in our Framingham plant. Servant leadership is not abdication of leadership; it is helping people figure out what each one needs to do.
>
> The ironic thing about power is you never really have it as a "thing in itself." You only have what people are willing to give you. Once we were deciding who should lead a particular team, and we had two candidates. One person was more technically talented, and the other had greater people skills and emotional literacy. We took a long time discussing the two of them, but eventually we got down to the central question: "Who would the team members most willingly follow?" Once we asked that question, it provided the answer we needed about who should lead the team. Another good question for a leader is if he is willing to follow. There will be times when a leader needs to give up power and let a person with special knowledge or talent take over. In picking a leader, you should choose someone who is able to give up power when needed.
>
> —Rob Zicaro

As with other paradoxes in this book, when a leader becomes effective by helping, not controlling, his or her strength as a leader grows. We can take a lesson from politicians. Russell Long was one of the most powerful Senators ever. He used that power to pass legislation for employee ownership plans, among a lot of other things. According to people who worked with him, Long's real strength was that he never missed an opportunity to do a favor. Later on, he could get those "chits" paid back. Leaders in business are in much the same situation. If they help other people to do their jobs, the people will be more willing to help them carry out their leadership roles.

But how specifically can a leader act as a servant? One way, of course, is to listen to people. Go out among the people and ask what they need to do their jobs better. Do they need different tools? Do they need new information resources? Do they need their work space laid out differently? Some of these requests you will not be able to fill, but many you will. People will do their work better, and you will gain more respect as someone who delivers.

Servant leaders also work to eliminate unnecessary bureaucratic rules and procedures that hinder people taking responsible action. Do all those reports really need to be permanently filed? Do that many layers of management really need to sign off on something for action to be taken? Can employees be given their own budget for making certain decisions?

Servant leaders also look for things that could make people's jobs easier. Perhaps people should be sent to special training programs. Perhaps there needs to be new rules for flex time or family leave. Perhaps the company needs to share more financial information with people, or information measuring how individual jobs are done.

These and other possibilities make it clear that being a servant leader is more, not less, demanding of special managerial skills. As in all these paradoxes, helping other people take responsibility is itself the most challenging kind of responsibility a leader can assume.

Paradox 8

WE CORRECT BETTER THROUGH GRACE THAN THROUGH CONFRONTATION.

To this point, it might seem that I am arguing that the role of the leader is to make it possible for everyone else to make decisions. That is only partly true. Leaders need to know when to say no. While these circumstances should eventually become rare (and there should be a willingness to let people make some noncritical errors as a learning experience or to build credibility that you will let people make decisions), there will be times when a leader is certain that an employee is taking the wrong approach. In these cases, leaders have to correct some people. But how they do it is vital. When you correct through grace, people feel effective and built up. You allow them to be their better selves and correct themselves.

Webster defines grace as "The quality or state of being considerate or thoughtful; a disposition to or an act or instance of kindness or clemency." That is really too simple an explanation. A state of grace is a sense of rightness with the world or, in a spiritual sense, with God. We can help people find grace by how we make them feel, not just about themselves, but how they fit into the work world we share with them.

Let me try to explain what I mean by correcting through grace—a distinctly religious concept—by describing something that happened to me when I was a preacher in the early 1970s. I was preaching for the Clinton Boulevard Church of Christ in Jackson, Mississippi. I was proud of my preaching but I had to overcome fear every time I preached. I was preaching just after the schools had been forcibly integrated. All the people in my congregation had pulled their kids out of public school and put them into the Council School. I later realized the name of the school was White Citizens' Council School.

I preached several sermons on racism, none of which was received well. After I used the phrase "black lady" in one of my sermons an elderly lady said to me, "Charles, you don't know this, but Negro women aren't ladies." I took her to task for being a racist. I asked her what it would take for her to see Negroes as real people. I challenged her beliefs and upset her sense of rightness with the world. Her feelings were hurt—she thought I did not understand, and she really let me know it. I did understand, because my parents had grown up in the South too.

When I was challenging her beliefs head on, I could see her stop listening to me. Her eyes disengaged from mine. I realized I needed to change my approach, and abandon confrontation in favor of grace. I asked her simple questions that got her to pay attention to me again. I asked her three questions: What have Negroes done to you? Do you know any Negroes personally? Do you have friends that are Negroes? On reflection she said she had some friends who were Negroes. One swept her house and washed her clothes every day. Another worked at the corner grocery. What kind of people are they? She said they're not bad people at all. I talked to her about her Negro friends and she lightened up about them. Now she could see that perhaps there was a way to look at things differently that came out of her own experiences. She could feel right with her world, even if her view of it had hopefully changed some, because I had tried to bring her around based on her own insights.

I had this experience in the plant too. I have noted throughout this book how in my early management experience I sometimes tended to think I knew the best way to do something and really did not want to listen to anyone else. I was dismissive of anyone who challenged my point of view. I was careless with the feelings of other people; I did not give them grace. Not surprisingly, people were not eager to follow my wishes. I was a leader in the plant, but I did not have much influence with a lot of people. I learned, however, that when I asked someone in a way that did not demand they do it, they responded more amiably. Eventually, they were no longer afraid of me. When approached as colleagues in a respectful, considerate way, people do not have to be defensive about everything. They can experiment more because they do not have to worry about negative consequences.

If someone does something wrong, assume the best. It may be that he has merely misunderstood the situation and done what he thought best, given his mistaken information. In this case, the solution is easy. Once you recognize that a person has made a factual mistake, provide them with a true understanding of the situation, and they will be equipped to make the right decision the next time.

But if someone rebels against your authority then the problem is not just poor information. We are tempted to fire these people. This is a natural human reflex. But managers should always try to remember that no one sets out to be a jerk. The person may have been poisoned in a previous life or a previous job. This rebellion is her instinct, not willful action. When a manager chastises or threatens to fire such an employee, it reinforces the poisoning of her spirit.

When I was running a plant in Atlanta, I assigned someone the task of taking out the garbage everyday. He did not want to do it. He saw it as beneath his dignity. But he was a new employee and I had to have him do this. He was not skilled in any of the other things our plant does, such as machine operations. I tried scolding him. This led to our going separate ways. Today, I would handle the situation differently. I would try to get him to understand why the trash needed to be dumped. I would build more significance in this job. Even though it is a dirty job, I could have emphasized the contribution this job makes. And, as implied in other parts of this book, the path to take is to get him to think through the issues involved in trash removal by asking him questions rather than giving him a lecture on plant cleanliness.

Let's be honest though. You can and should give grace to employees, but not every employee will work out. You are not being fair to other employees who are trying to build a sense of teamwork if you persist in retaining someone who insists on rebelling. In that case, you may be, in fact, acting as an arrogant manager so sure of his or her ability to bring out the best in people that you cannot accept that sometimes nothing will work.

We read a lot these days about tough managers. Al "Chainsaw" Dunlap said you do not need friends as a manager—if you need friends, he said, get a dog. He has two. I think Dunlap and people who share his approach are going down the wrong path to create profits. But I also think there is more to work than making money, and I think almost no one really believes that making money is all that matters at work. Human beings need a sense that they are contributing to other people's lives. They need a feeling of community. They need a feeling that other people wish them well. In short, they need grace.

Grace is a basic human need we recognize in the rest of our lives—I believe it is shortsighted to assume that it is not important at work. Peter Block said in his book *Stewardship* that "What harsh reality made clear was that hope and optimism were sometimes irrelevant and that compliance and fitting in counted." I would not want to live a life without hope and optimism. I do not think many of you reading this book would either.

~

Mukesh was a production manager in our Atlanta plant. He was compassionate, but he had an odd habit of asking people rather blunt questions out of the blue. He had not mastered the ethic of gently raising issues. Even though he had a kind manner, he confronted people by asking questions. He had a way of asking questions with no preamble or greeting or context—questions that sometimes insulted people and made their mistakes seem ominous.

I spoke with him regularly about this. For the longest time he did not understand. He needed some mentoring, which I had not done. So I talked with him every day before he started his shift and warned him about his style of asking questions. I asked questions like "Why did X get upset when you asked him an innocent question? Why was his response so harsh?" I did not ask him the same type of question that he asked others. I helped him to understand that if his boss, me, were to ask him those types of questions, he would get upset too. I did not tell him that his style of questioning was wrong; I helped him over time to see that his reaction to these questions would be the same as his subordinates. By nature he is an encourager, but for some reason this did not get expressed in the way he asked people things. "Just the facts," was how it came across. Now everybody respects him. They cannot do enough to please him. His tone of voice, the context-setting for the questions, it is all different now.

Paradox 9

WE GAIN RESPECT NOT BY DEMANDING IT, BUT BY GIVING IT.

Everyone wants to be respected, but there are different kinds of respect.

In street lingo, respect may really mean fear. Odd, but that is often management lingo too. On the street, this kind of respect may come at the end of a gun, a knife, or the right "attitude." In the plant, it may come as the threat of pink slip or demotion, or maybe just a chewing out in front of friends.

Another type of respect is for people's technical capabilities, accomplishments, and skills. There are athletes whose skills we all respect, but whom we may not much admire as people. In the plant, there are managers who clearly have tremendous skills, but who have little real rapport with workers because they are respected only for their knowledge.

Then there is a deeper respect, the respect for people's values and principles. We all respected Mother Theresa; some of us deeply respected Martin Luther King for his commitment to racial justice, while others respected Strom Thurmond for his opposition to many of the principles Dr. King articulated. Because our values are so individual, our respect for people based on these values may be limited to a fairly narrow range of people.

Each of these different kinds of respect is limited; we can give it to only people who possess certain attributes. There is, however, a deeper respect, the respect for every human being simply because they are human. It is the kind of respect referred to by the United States' founding fathers when they said, "All men are created equal." They did not mean everyone was the same, but that all men were equal with respect to certain inalienable rights. In the plant, that principle tells us that we must respect the rights of every worker as a person. We must be considerate of his needs for a sense of accomplishment, importance, challenge, and security.

If we approach everyone this way, I believe we will receive that same kind of respect. That does not mean that I cannot challenge someone's ideas, but that she can also challenge mine. It does not mean that, if needed, I cannot take disciplinary action against someone who does not meet the company's standards, but I do have to explain it thoroughly and show the person how to change to achieve his and our goals.

This type of respect is not objective. Demanding that people respect us as a whole person is impossible—demanding such respect proves that we do not deserve it. It demonstrates a need for external validation that shows insecurity or arrogance. When we act in a way that respects people, it shows that we are strong leaders and that we are worthy of respect. We gain respect by being honorable and honest, by treating people like people. We can look at all of these characteristics—honesty, expressing vulnerability, listening, and responding sincerely—as how we manifest our respect for others.

~

When I first moved to Massachusetts to be part of the corporate staff, I had just been made Vice President for Manufacturing. One Sunday, I drove past the Framingham plant on the way to my office in Westborough and I saw a couple of cars parked in the parking lot. I said to myself, "Evidently something is going on today." That was the first time I met Calvin.

I introduced myself to him and asked him how he was doing. I had trouble getting a conversation going with him. I was probably rattling along looking for something that would energize him and missed the mark. I am a strong advocate of employee ownership, so I must have been talking about employee ownership. Suddenly he stopped me in mid-sentence and said, "Are you serious? I'm 50 years old and don't have a lot more chances to invest in something else."

Cal was working on Saturday because he had volunteered his machine as an overflow machine—if he did not work on a Saturday, a customer's order would not go out on time.

I took it as a matter of conscience to prove that I was serious in honoring Cal's commitment. This is the leading edge of leadership. "Are you serious?" That is a question everyone wants to know the answer to. I proved I was serious by getting him involved in employee ownership. I helped him become a champion of the idea by sending him to some national conferences. At one point he made a presentation at the national ESOP Association conference. He got everybody's attention.

Paradox 10

WE LEARN BY TALKING, NOT JUST BY LISTENING.

After reading that, you may be thinking, "Now wait a minute, Charles. The very first paradox in this book is that we have more influence when we listen than when we tell. Now you say we need to talk more. Which is it?"

It's both. Listening expands our *influence;* talking expands our *knowledge.* It is a simple principle, really. When we have to express something in our own words, we learn it better. It is not just passive knowledge any more. The best way to master something is to teach it.

If you can get people to repeat key ideas back to you, they will understand better. You do not want them to just parrot back your own words, however. Perhaps they should be asked to think about it and come back to you the next day and explain it as they see it. Or, even better, have them explain it to someone else, then ask that person to explain it to you. You can, if needed, correct the second person, who can take it back to the first person, who can come back to you. This chain of learning can go on indefinitely. You could do the same thing with any group of three people in your organization. One way we commonly see this is in teaching basic business literacy. At Smith and Company, an employee-owned engineering company in Missouri, people were just not understanding the financial presentations. Then the president, Sam Smith, decided to ask a different employee to explain the month's financial report each time. Eventually, everyone has the task, and now they really understand the numbers.

Talking can also help us get into other people's heads. As leaders, we have a passive understanding when employees describe something to us. But if we can say something to someone else in words that he would approve of, we have a very solid understanding of his position. What's more important, when we can describe ideas to another person's satisfaction, she feels understood and knows we have heard her. When people feel that you have really heard them this way, you will have gained a strong measure of their respect and willingness to trust you.

I saw this firsthand once when I was trying to explain a particular production function at work to some people on the floor. They did not understand it and I had to leave to take care of another matter. Later on, when I got back to them, they no longer needed my help. They had figured it out themselves. What had happened? They had to explain it to other people who worked there. To this day I still have no idea how they learned it well enough to explain it to others. They accepted the responsibility and collectively worked out the solution.

At our company, we have always insisted that people from the front line communicate various aspects of plant news and operations. All of these people become champions of "their" issue. Employee ownership is one example. They are able to explain some of the technical issues of ESOPs to their co-workers. Employee ownership is often misunderstood in our company. People who emerged as its champions contribute significantly to the overall understanding of our ESOP among all employees.

One principle of our orientation program is that machine operators should do some of the training. We set up a series of ten lessons for the orientation program, covering all aspects of the plant and its operations. Operators led the training and taught most of the segments. We saw them get more enthusiastic about their jobs as their understanding increased. They have become champions of the process. We also have managers teach some of the segments, generally the ones on employee-ownership and overall plant philosophy. It was exciting for me to see the plant management's growing enthusiasm for ownership and the new management style we were trying to build.

> The orientation program, which involved people from all parts of the company, sets a unique context for the incoming employees. They know it's a special company. The last group we did it for, we tried to hire several people at the same time so we could put them through the program together. They liked seeing several people from different parts of the company.
>
> —*Rob Zicaro*

Paradox 11

WITH PEOPLE, THE SHORTEST DISTANCE BETWEEN TWO POINTS IS NOT A STRAIGHT LINE.

This paradox is really about the perspective that you take when you need to direct or correct someone. If you look at the issue as being one of solving an immediate problem, the shortest distance (that is, the simplest solution) may be a straight line: You just tell your subordinate what to do. You force her to do it without understanding why. She serves as an extension of you.

But if you take a longer-term perspective, the real problem is that your subordinate was not able or not willing to solve the problem. If you are trying to get from point A to point B, it is a question of whether point A is "job X has not been done" or "Joe is not able or willing to do job X correctly." And the point B you really want to get to is to get Joe to do the job right next time, and all the times the problem arises in the future. Maybe that involves making sure that Joe has the motivation to do the job right. Maybe it involves assuring he has the ability to do it. In either case, it is a much more difficult task for you as a leader than just telling Joe what to do.

One way you can encourage Joe to have the motivation to do the job right is to get him to talk through the importance of the job. You can give Joe the ability to do the job right by helping him work through the objectives and challenges in completing the job. Have him do this out loud with you, and he will eventually come to a workable solution (albeit sometimes with a lot of coaching from you). And because of your investment in him, he will have a greater ability, and a greater motivation, to solve future problems.

People want to be trusted. Having your subordinates work out solutions in front of you and implement them indicates the degree of your trust in them, and your trust in their ability to solve problems on their own.

Paradox 12

THE HARD STUFF IS THE SOFT STUFF.

Tom Peters said, "Business would be easy if it weren't for all the damn people." We could design elegant participation systems and, zap, the company would be participative. It doesn't work that way. As a friend once told me about child care books, "The problem with the advice they give you is that when you try it in real life, the kids don't know their lines." The same thing is true in management. The books tell you "do this," and people will "say that." No they won't, at least not right away. It takes time, and it takes nurturing. People need to be taught to use new sources of information. They need to learn to work in groups by trying it with easy things first. They need active encouragement and lots of feedback. Most of all, managers need to understand that change is difficult, especially if it is change that introduces more responsibility and more ambiguity to a job. To make these new systems effective, management needs to be able to deal with these very human emotions in people, to be able to pay attention to the soft stuff.

The "soft stuff" means dealing with the human side of management. It means relating to people as people, not dealing with them as objects, as instruments to perform a task. Managers have a tendency to focus on things they can measure and capture in numerical format. They look at financial statements, machine tolerances, and inventory turns. It is more difficult to deal with emotional issues. That would be OK, if we were not emotional beings before we were rational beings. Bert Decker made an important point in his book, *You Have To Be Believed To Be Heard.* In it he says, "People buy on emotion and justify with fact . . . . We in effect decide (or 'buy') at that level and then use our intellect to justify our decisions."

The soft stuff is difficult because people are difficult. They are complicated and they have emotions, which are frequently irrational and self-contradictory. For this reason alone, the soft stuff is hard. There is simply more to it.

But this is complicated by the fact that many managers are inappropriately trained to manage people. They have technical skills, and they may well have come up through the ranks of employees. No business school course in human resources management or organizational psychology, however well intentioned, well designed, and well taught, can possibly prepare a manager for the depth and complexity of a real world human organization. People often take the path of least resistance, even if it is a subconscious choice, and focus on the areas in which they have the most confidence and experience. The result is managers who neglect the soft side of management and who neglect the development of their own abilities to manage people.

One time in the Framingham plant we redesigned the operating structure into teams. Teams ended up not working there. We began with a good effort, which combined nurturing of individuals with responsibilities that were gradually shared with the work force. Eventually, as the process continued after I left the plant, there began to be a divergence between the responsibilities and the nurturing. People were given responsibilities before they were ready. One of my best friends at the plant quit because he was discouraged about the changes.

One common problem companies encounter when they move to a more participative management style is over-enthusiasm: Perhaps they learned what some other company is doing and tried to import that system in one piece. But there is important groundwork to be done. Management may not be ready to give up its prerogatives. Employees may be intimidated and confused by all the new responsibility. Information systems may not be in place to give people the data and feedback they need to make the new system work. You can deal with this problem by spending months or years preparing people for a radical change, or you can take a more practical approach and start with a few steps, expanding as you go along. I think in retrospect, we would have been better off at Framingham if we had viewed teams as the goal, not as a single, very big step.

But the story does not even stop there. The way to manage people, the soft stuff, is the main focus of this book. As we have talked about, managing people well involves understanding, at a deep and reflexive level, the paradoxes of leadership. It involves very difficult tasks: honesty, listening, respecting, nurturing, and expressing vulnerability. The only way to undertake these tasks is to make a personal commitment to living them. The only way out of the horns of these paradoxes is through the soul. We must hold the value of the people we work with as a central focus of our intuition, of our waking thought, of our attention while we are at work, and when we are away from work. To be competent with soft stuff, we must look into ourselves. Deeply. We must find where we are close to the ideals we aspire to and where we need to face our weaknesses and overcome them.

One way we pay attention to the soft stuff is by helping people to understand and tackle the hard stuff—the financial numbers, the production routines, the problem solving techniques. Survey after survey shows that what people value most about their job is not pay, or even security, but challenge, a sense of being able to use their skills fully, and a sense of working for something important. If we can help people take on larger issues at work, we greatly increase the chances that our employees will be motivated to do a great job.

Perhaps one of the most difficult aspects of managing the "soft stuff" is how to deal with passive employees. Treat even these employees as talented, well-intentioned people who have the ability and the motivation to do the work of the company well. Entrust them with the responsibility to perform meaningful tasks of importance to the success of the company. This accomplishes two goals: It puts more of the work of the company into their hands and frees managers from mundane tasks. It also demonstrates the trust that you feel in them. It improves their morale and makes them feel like valuable employees. People rise or fall to our expectations of them.

Paradox 13

SOMETIMES WE HAVE TO GET IT WRONG TO GET IT RIGHT.

We learn by celebrating our mistakes. No one gets it right all the time. In fact, we all have to get it wrong sometimes to bring out the best ideas. Warren Bennis points out that one CEO told him that if she had a knack for leadership, it was the capacity to make as many mistakes as she could as soon as possible, and thus get them out of the way. We have to experiment with some things that do not turn out well. In fact, these can look like failures, but the response to your failures is to recognize that no one gets it right all the time. Experiments are necessary to build victories. Sometimes you have to get it wrong to get it right.

Businesses today have to be innovative, responsive, and creative to survive. That means they have to take risks; they have to try things that may not always work. A business that never makes a mistake is almost certainly one that is too conservative, too careful. One of the ways this willingness to take risks shows itself is letting people take on more responsibility than they would in conventional organizations. There is the risk, of course, that they will not always do the right thing, but the greater risk is that by not having the authority to do more, the organization will miss out on a lot of useful ideas, creative responses to customers, more efficient ways of doing things, and many other contributions people can make if they have the chance.

If the atmosphere of the organization is "Don't make errors," then people, even if they technically have decision-making authority, will be hesitant to step forward. After all, people usually do not get punished for failing to be innovative, but they may get reprimanded for making errors. The key is to let people make mistakes, but use them as learning opportunities. Mistakes are the greatest teaching tool you can have; people have both the specific reference and the motivation to learn to do something better.

At Reflexite, an employee-owned company in Connecticut, employees can submit suggestions through an elaborate and effective employee involvement system. Employees have to fill out a form with their ideas; the form helps them walk through how the idea can be developed. If the idea is not used, someone from the employee involvement committee, or a supervisor, has to help them understand exactly why it was not. It is a great learning opportunity. It is also important to encourage people to come up with ideas, even if they are rejected.

In most of our life, we think that if we only succeed two times out ten, we have failed (especially in school!). But in business, two out of ten is pretty good. The eight ideas you do not use will require relatively little time. But the two ideas that are used might save the company enormous time or money. Think about it. Isn't it true for most businesses that what really sets them apart is a few really good ideas about how to do things differently and better? Wouldn't it be great to get more good ideas? If you discourage people from coming up with ideas by frowning too much on mistakes, you are going to miss a lot of these potential turning points.

In fact, we should *celebrate* mistakes. Quad/Graphics, a major employee-owned printing company in Wisconsin, has an annual event at which the year's worst mistakes are honored. Quad/Graphics management knows that mistakes are the key to knowledge. They are how we learn, and more important, how we learn how to learn.

Warren Bennis, in his book *Why Leaders Can't Lead,* says "Leaders make it clear that there is no failure, only mistakes that give us feedback and tell us what to do next." Of course, some mistakes are dangerous. You need to be careful about the ones that can sink the whole company. At W.L. Gore, the employee-owned manufacturer of Gore-Tex, employees are empowered to make any decision their team supports, except where an error would be "below the waterline" and sink the ship. But too many managers, pressed by ego, do not even acknowledge making simple mistakes. They have to be right all the time.

There are three reactions to a mistake. The first one is defensiveness—"It wasn't really my fault." The second response is pointing out other's mistakes. The third, and most mature, reaction is accepting the mistakes that we have made.

If leaders make mistakes, and do not defend them, they have more influence. John F. Kennedy was never as popular as when he went on national television and said he made a mistake in the Bay of Pigs. Bill Clinton has gotten himself into trouble by not being more forthcoming about the mistakes he has made. I know the temptation to cover up a mistake. Once I promised a customer that one of our machines could run on a type of material for which it actually was unsuited. As a result of my mistake, we lost the customer. I confessed to the whole plant and apologized to the people. At first people were angry because of losing the customer. But after this first reaction, they gave me grace because they knew I intended to do the right thing. This incident gave me more credibility.

The Final Paradox

A FULL LIFE IS ACHIEVED NOT BY GRASPING BUT BY GIVING.

"The perfection of man lies not in what man has, but in what man is."
—Oscar Wilde

It seems especially true in modern society that we have become a nation obsessed by grasping for more—more power, more money, more prestige. It is a losing battle, however, because however much of these things we get, someone else always has more, and we always compare ourselves to these "betters." That is perhaps why even though people are much more affluent today than ever before, they reported much higher levels of life satisfaction in the 1950s. When people are asked whom they most admire, they mention the Mother Theresas of the world. But when they think about whether they want their children to choose that life style, they are not so sure. When people are asked what they value most in life, they talk about family, friends, community, and a sense of purpose. But when we observe what they do as a measure of what they value, the focus somehow switches to consuming, competing, and trying to get more.

I once heard someone say that when we consider what is important to us, we should ask what we want to be remembered for. Few people would say, "For my fancy clothes, my big house, my extraordinary power, or my great looks." Instead, they would talk about how they want to be thought of as a good friend or parent, or perhaps someone who made a difference in other people's lives.

It seems, though, that our grasping nature is almost reflexive, the result of a simple, preconscious desire to possess. Giving, on the other hand, is a much more difficult process, requiring understanding of the person who is receiving our gift, as well as what we mean by giving it. Developing this knowledge is one of the sources of the richness of our lives.

There are tortured souls that think a full life is achieved by grasping. That is backwards. We do not *grasp* a full life. We live a full life by being the best person we can be. And the better we are, the more we give to others.

> *If I can ease one life the aching*
> *Or cool one pain,*
> *or help one fainting robin*
> *unto his nest again,*
> *I shall not live in vain.*
>
> —Emily Dickinson

As you read through this book, you may have thought to yourself: Why bother? You can undertake all the difficult introspective work we talk about here, or you can leave it alone. Either way, your salary will be the same. Your prospects for promotions may not change . . . . So why bother?

This final paradox is about that question. The salary and the job title you hold are of secondary importance. I have been thinking about this a lot lately: I have a degenerative illness that will shorten my life and which has helped me to focus on what matters. This book is an effort to put down what seems most important to me.

The process of writing this book has reinforced the notion about how to live a full life. While writing, I have thought back over many of the things I have done in my life. As I relive these events, I have a sense of what has made my life fuller, what parts of my life I have built toward the person I want to be, toward the life I want to live. And it is the times when I was able to give something to another person, to touch something inside them, to make a difference in their lives, that have contributed to my own life. The accomplishments, the promotions, the awards—these are important things. But these accomplishments mostly matter to the extent that they signify things I have given to others. They are not ends in themselves. Now that my world has narrowed, what I have is what I have given.

> *What do we live for, if it is not to make life less difficult for each other?*
>
> —George Eliot

In closing, I want to return to a couple of the paradoxes. They are the ones that speak most personally to me these days, and they deal mostly with vulnerability.

I am in one of the most dependent and vulnerable positions an adult can be in. Without my wife or my home health aides, I could not eat or drink, move from one place to another, or manage my medical needs. I cannot read books or adjust the thermostat. I cannot get out of bed by myself or tie my own shoes. I cannot type or write: The ideas you are reading are mine, but the hand that typed them is someone else's.

I am struggling with my illness now. Yet I am stronger now that I am vulnerable. Lots of people reach out to help me these days, even strangers in airports. I used to refuse people's help. I wanted to do everything by myself, and I wanted to be the one to give. I cannot do that any more, yet I feel stronger, not weaker. For one thing, the way I have handled my disease, people tell me, has inspired them. I am deeply touched by that.

But it is more than that, for I have learned new sources of strength precisely from the limitations of my disease. For instance, I used to talk very quickly. I already knew exactly what I was going to say, so I did not have to wait for the ideas to come. I just had to get the ideas out of my mouth as quickly as possible. If my disease disappeared tomorrow, I would continue to speak more slowly. I would talk less and listen more. Talking more slowly is one benefit of my disease. The time to write this book is another.

My fourth paradox reads "Even when we are effective, we still doubt ourselves." For much of my adult life, I have struggled with the tension between self-doubt, on one hand, and effectiveness as a leader on the other. I think that no honest, introspective leader ever fully transcends this tension. I have not. I was getting more comfortable with the tension—bearing it like a familiar burden—when my disease changed my perspective.

The doubt I feel now is not about my leadership abilities—it is a more substantial and more profound doubt than any I ever felt as a company manager. Before I may have doubted my ability to accomplish a specific task or my worthiness to be a leader. Now I cannot trust my body. The doubt I feel about myself today touches fundamental parts of my self-conception. Thomas Jefferson wept on stage when he felt his life had been a failure. In some ways, this book is a way for me to make my tears public.

"We are stronger when we are vulnerable." I am convinced that this paradox is true for the types of vulnerability a leader faces. But I do not know if this paradox applies to the type of vulnerability I am experiencing now. How can physical limitations make me stronger?

Now I have admitted to you my vulnerabilities and my self-doubts. My mind, and my hopes, tell me that it is still possible for me to be strong, for me to affect people's lives for the better. If my tears express weakness, perhaps they contain strength as well. This book, and its effect on you, will be a test of the strength of vulnerability. I hope you will find something of truth in these paradoxes, something that speaks to you. The real test of my words, the test I am most scared of, is their ability to get from your head, where they are now, into your heart.

I imagine that every author has this hope. Perhaps this book feels different to me only because it is my book. But I hope that you will read these words and strive to make them yours. I give these paradoxes to you, the reader of this book. Maybe giving is all I can ask, but I hope that you will receive them. Receiving the paradoxes is an active task. It requires soul-searching. It requires breaking deeply rooted habits. It requires vulnerability.

So here is one final vulnerability of mine: I want this book to change your life, and I do not know if it can.

Reflections

Reflections

LOREN RODGERS

National Center for Employee Ownership (formerly with Ownership Associates)

I came into Charles' life about the same time as his disease did. I had just moved to a new town, to a new job, and was starting my post-graduate professional career. I had found a job that let me work exactly how I wanted to do: employee ownership. Having a dream come true is a bit unnerving. What if it turns out to be less than you had hoped?

One part of my new career in Boston was to serve as the administrator for the New England Chapter of the ESOP Association, of which Charles was Chapter President. That made him my boss, I suppose, although it never felt like that. My impression, which sounds self-contradictory, was that Charles would never express disappointment in me, but that he would not tolerate performance which fell below his (quite high) standards.

Charles helped mentor me into my new career. He solicited my ideas and responded in a way that made it clear he heard and appreciated them. He did not always agree, but he often found a way to get me to come to a revised conclusion myself. Charles also helped me out in some very concrete ways. He personally advanced me my first month's salary and offered me the use of his car.

When I first met him, no symptoms were noticeable. Soon after, a few small things happened—things I did not attach any importance to, but looking back I can see it was the disease. For example, sometimes when he turned to look at me, Charles' eyes would pass me, and then gradually re-focus on my face. Once, driving back to Boston together, we ran out of gas. I now know that Charles was concentrating so hard on the road that he did not notice the gas meter.

Charles has been working on this book for a long time. His notes go back for years. I started working with him in early 1998, with the goal of helping him get his ideas down on paper. At that point, Charles could no longer type, so I came over every week or so and took dictation. Charles would talk, and I got down as much as I could. Charles said that he could tell from the sound of the keys that I type quickly—as usual, he was being generous. He knew what he wanted to say, and I did my best to get down what I could.

Over the months, that gradually changed. Charles often worked with Cindy Waldron, his health aide at the office. She helped get his ideas and words down on paper. My job was to take what they wrote and fit it into the rest of the text. I also typed what Charles said, but now I could keep up. And my typing had not gotten faster.

Later still, the disease began to affect Charles' short- and medium-term memory. We were still writing, still adding to the text, but the style was different. Charles and I had conversations. I would look through the text, see where there was a hole, and ask him a question. His answer would fill the hole. Sometimes, when he got stuck, I would suggest a possible next word for the sentence, and that would get him going again—whether he agreed or not, he'd be off again, spinning his sentences. Other times, someone would come in and all three of us would work together. Rob Zicaro, June Sekera, and Calvin Arey in particular would come in and we would all talk—good things would come from those conversations. Parts of them are in this book.

As Charles' disease progressed, the focus of his writing narrowed. He has read thousands of books and has spoken with thousands of people. He draws quotations, analysis, anecdotes, and wisdom from a rich variety of experiences, people, and authors. Gradually, he lost access to those internal sources. As the scope of memories and ideas he could draw on narrowed, he kept coming back to particular themes: We listen through the filter of our fear, we are emotional beings before we are rational beings, and less is more. Maybe it is a weakness that the breadth of material we talk about has decreased, but it is also a strength: His focus has intensified on what he sees as most important. To a large extent, that means the paradoxes themselves.

Toward the end of writing the text, I had trouble understanding his speech, and Charles had trouble retrieving the memories he was looking for. Once in a while, with the few remaining gaps, I would type up a paragraph or two and read it to Charles. He would either say he liked it, or it went back to the drawing board.

As other people, myself included, gradually became involved in the basic tasks of writing this book, I think we began to feel a sense of community. As Charles' senses gradually fail him, he is becoming more isolated from the world. It is yet one more paradox that this isolation has created a community. As his voice becomes more difficult to understand, a multitude of other voices, some of which are on the next several pages, have taken its place.

Charles, however, is the author of this book. He is the center of this community. People in his community share many similar ideas—partly that is because we all have overlapping values and beliefs, but it is also partly because of Charles. We have all learned from Charles and are better people because of him.

As you read through the fourteen paradoxes, you'll hear Charles' own words. As you read through the text written by other people, you will hear Charles' words again, this time through the memory of each of the other writers. I know that I use phrases that feel natural and obvious, and only after they are out of my mouth do I realize I got them from Charles. As you read through the following pages, you will see lots of references to things Charles said or conversations the writer had with Charles. His words have become part of the lives of the people in this community.

There are many more people who could have written, and many more people who have their own stories of how Charles lived the paradoxical life of a leader. For those of you who know Charles, you will hear his voice echoing through the beautiful and evocative reflections that follow. You will be reminded of the ideas and the perspectives that tie our Charles-centered community together. For those of you who have not met Charles, this book, and the reflections that follow, are an invitation to join us.

Reflections

BOB FULTON
Chairman of Web Industries

About 20 years ago a young doctoral candidate came to work for Web Industries. His intention was to obtain an income while completing his work for a Doctorate in Philosophy at Boston University. Thus, while teaching Intro to Ethics at Salem State and Bridgewater State and working on his doctorate, he began working part time at Web Converting of Framingham. Not long after coming to work for Web he approached me about the possibility of working for Web full time. He had concluded that the academic world of philosophy was not for him—Web had given him a taste of the marketplace and he was excited about investing himself in it.

Because I had gotten to know Charles Edmunson and the talented capable person that he was, I suggested that he begin a job search. I did not feel that Web had the opportunity and challenge that would satisfy Charles. After he pounded the pavement for a while and the two of us continued to interact, he said that he was convinced that he wanted to work at Web. The values, atmosphere, and culture of Web had captured him and he simply wanted to become part of the company and contribute to its values and growth. To say that we acquired a very special person would be an understatement. Charles has made more of an impact on people during his time at Web than anyone. His love and availability for everyone soon became well known.

Charles began his career with Web Industries, Inc., at the Framingham plant. After learning a bit about machine operation, he became a department foreman and then shift supervisor. Charles was always looking for more to do. He was constantly thinking of new ways of communicating and training, and new means of helping people reach their potential. Whatever his job was, people always came first. As one might expect, this took a lot of his time, but to him that just meant working extra hours to complete his own tasks. Charles will be best remembered for all the encouragement and help he gave to so many.

When Web was putting a management team together for the new Atlanta plant, Charles was asked to accept the role of Sales Manager. This was a new role for Charles and one that he had little experience in but he stepped up to the plate and did an excellent job helping the plant grow. During this time I spent a great deal of time with him and our friendship continued to deepen.

Charles soon became General Manager of the Atlanta plant. It was during this time that we built a new facility in Atlanta. In addition to his "people time" and running the plant, Charles also served as the onsite company construction manager. A number of times he attempted to fit in work on an MBA, but his other activities simply got in the way—as important as education was to him, it did not rate high enough for him to pull it off. But at one point he found out about the Georgia State MBA program and asked if this might be the right place and time for him to get serious. I encouraged him to apply, but told him that if he was accepted he would no longer be able to run the plant at the same time. I assured him that we would provide some challenging opportunities while he was working for his MBA. This was a disappointment to him but he accepted it and went on to help his team do well at Georgia State and receive his MBA.

After completing his MBA, he and Janet once again moved to Boston, as Charles accepted the role of VP Manufacturing. As time went on we realized that his title might better have been VP People. The encouragement and growth of people has been Charles' greatest contribution. Whether it was at Web, the ESOP Association, or any other area, he contributed greatly, and his love for people was his guiding light.

During 1996, Charles and Janet were in London and visited my daughter and son-in-law, Todd and Donna Pihl. Todd noticed that Charles had difficulty while going down the stairs to the tube. On returning home, Charles got eyeglasses, thinking that would help. It wasn't long after that the journey of Charles' disease began. He continued to contribute in whatever way he was able until January 1st this year (1999) when he retired and moved home. Those of us who receive his e-mail each day continue to be encouraged and challenged by his unending courage and determination.

Last week I had the opportunity to read a draft of Charles' *Paradoxes of Leadership*. As each of the fourteen paradoxes have been lived out in his life, we too have been drawn to experiment and learn to live out these paradoxes as well. They need to be deeply rooted in all of our relationships.

Surprisingly, these paradoxes resonate with the Bible, a book that he knew very well and used during his time as a minister. To highlight a few: Paradox 1 is reflected in "Everyone should be quick to listen, slow to speak" (James 1:19). Paradox 5 is in 2 Corinthians 12:10 when the Apostle Paul says, "When I am weak then I am strong." Paradox 7 is best expressed by Jesus in Mark 10:43, "Whoever wants to be first among you must be your servant." In Paradox 8 Charles says, "A state of grace is a sense of rightness with the world or, in a spiritual sense, with God"—again, the Apostle Paul perhaps says it best in Ephesians 2:8–9, "For by grace you have been made right with God through faith not by what we have done but it is a gift from God." It seems to me that once a person experiences this, then they are compelled to express grace in all of their relationships.

> *Amazing grace, how sweet the sound*
> *That saved a wretch like me!*
> *I once was lost, but now am found,*
> *Was blind, but now can see.*
> —John Newton

All preachers need to be reminded that we must practice what we preach. Charles did this. May each of us seek to practice the essence of these fourteen paradoxes. In this way, Charles will continue to be a blessing to many.

Reflections

COREY ROSEN

National Center for Employee Ownership

I have spent the last 18 years talking to people about employee ownership and, as part of that, telling them what I thought I knew about managing. Many of the lessons were the same as Charles has described here, but they all had to do with finding ways to get employee owners more involved in sharing their ideas and information. Naturally, I thought that I needed to "walk the talk" in my own organization. I had the form down just right. Every week, we met to discuss any issue anyone wanted to raise. I considered it a matter of principle that any decision of any importance—hiring, new projects, spending more than a trivial amount of money, a new leave policy—had to be made with the input and consensus of everyone.

A funny thing happened, however. Our participative structure yielded consent, but not consensus. I would go into the meetings with a clear idea of what I wanted to do and what I thought the organization needed to do. Of course, I did not want to force people to accept this point of view, so I would start by framing the issue. Here are the pros and cons, I would say, of hiring someone, or of taking on this new project. As people said their piece, I would comment, often making my views pretty clear, but reiterating that this was a group decision. As Charles always used to say when he gave his inspiring speeches, "Guess what? People almost invariably ended up saying they agreed with me. What a great process! We had consensus, and I got to do what I wanted us to do."

Except we did not really have consensus, of course. We had consent. People figured out where I was coming from pretty quickly and figured, well, he is the boss, so I guess we might as well go along. Moreover, like a lot of managers, making verbal arguments is one of my strengths, so I might even convince people at the moment I was right (but not on reflection).

This proved corrosive in a variety of ways. First, one of the points of doing this was that if people felt the decision were theirs, they would carry it out with a lot more enthusiasm. But if all they were doing was consenting, it was not really theirs. In fact, they may have felt less enthused than if they were just told what to do because, at least some of the time, they may have felt manipulated. Second, people felt the organization did not always live up to its own ideals; lacking that, their commitment to stay was undermined. Most important, however, was that we were not really getting the benefit of people's ideas.

What changed this for me was one of the paradoxes Charles mentions, that sometimes we have to get it wrong to get it right. It was a simple issue that did the trick, really. For some years, I had argued that we could not afford to print our publications in the fancier format (like a bookstore book) that most of the staff had been arguing for. We would meet to discuss it, and end up agreeing not to do it for now. Eventually, one of the staff members just said, look, for this book, we are doing it this way! It looked great—and it sold a lot better. Moreover, people no doubt took its contents more seriously. Now all our publications look that way, and we sell a lot more books.

About the same time, I had pushed through a decision to hire someone who, it turned out, worked out very badly, causing some serious problems among the staff. Staff members insisted on a different, even more participative process in the future. We have not made anything but a great hire since.

Well, I thought, I was really wrong on these things. What else could I be wrong on? I certainly didn't know. So now in meetings, I try to let other people speak first. I try very hard not to tip my hand, nor to frame the issue in a way that biases one view or another. If a consensus emerges, then I can just support it (even if I don't agree). If not, then, and only then, should I make my own argument. At first, I thought this would be a big risk, and that I would have to retain the power to veto something that I thought was a serious mistake. As it turns out, however, I have never had a strong disagreement with a staff decision since then, although there have been times when I went into a meeting with a different opinion than what I left it with, and, once in a great while, I feel there is something we just have to do, and I say that at the outset. I am sure I do not succeed at doing all this as well as I am describing it, but staff people tell me things are a lot truer to what we have been saying. Perhaps a better test is that people now stay at the NCEO a long time. We now have a staff of experienced, exceptionally competent people, all of whom can do their own jobs better than I could do them.

In fact, I can now pretty much avoid being a manager at all, and focus on the things that I like best and, hopefully, do the best. The organization has experienced exceptionally rapid growth since all this became effective, meaning we are able to reach far more people than ever before. My power as a manager of other people is, in some ways, less, but the irony is that my influence as the director of this organization has never been as great. I am also having more fun at work; it is a joy to go to work every day because of the people I work with. So, as Charles says, you gain power by giving it up.

My fear in relating this, especially after reading Charles' book, is that my saying it will sound arrogant, a kind of retrospective false modesty as a prelude to a great insight. I hope it does not come across this way. The truth is that I made some serious errors as a manager before, but, on the whole, I think I did pretty well. On the other hand, the insight I discuss here shouldn't have taken me so many years to have. Moreover, I am sure that my rhetoric is not always consistent with the reality at work. Charles talked about this tension too. He deeply believes he has some important insights to share (and he is right), but he wants to offer them in a spirit of humility. Charles always inspired people to act in this way; I can only hope to emulate that ultimate lesson of his.

Reflections

RICHARD DUFFY

Chapter Development Advisor to the ESOP Association; President of Ownership Visions

> *There is in the work of every great person, a distinctive and unmistakable, marked and individual manner, which identifies the man wherever a bit of his work appears.*
> —traditional saying

Those of us who have been fortunate enough to know and work with Charles Edmunson over the years understand upon reading his book, *Paradoxes of Leadership,* that it is not another theoretical treatise on leadership. Rather, his fourteen paradoxes are at their best an autobiographical reflection on the requisite leadership skills that Charles has experienced and learned while developing as an effective and successful leader.

I first encountered Charles some 10 years ago at the ESOP Association's Annual Conference in Washington D.C. His manner was easy and friendly and I recall my impression was that we were kindred spirits in the realm of ideas about the real value and potential power of this simple idea called employee ownership. Yet I must confess that the initial chance meeting left me also with the feeling that Charles was shy and unassuming . . . not one to rock the boat or unfurl the sails of change.

At this chance meeting I was introduced to Bob Fulton, CEO of employee-owned Web Industries, and Charles' boss. Although Charles worked directly for Bob, it was abundantly clear that theirs was a relationship significantly more than one of boss and subordinate. Over the years since that first meeting, I have observed the enabling power of that relationship . . . the coaching and mentoring and the personal growth for both resulting from it. Clearly it was based on trust, respect, love, and understanding—it functioned wondrously in both directions. Adult father and adult son would best describe it. They were mentor and coach to each other.

Over time it became clear to me that the key to this relationship was the openness and ability to influence each other that they both felt. The wonder of this relationship struck me later when I came to know that Charles was an ex-Christian minister who left the ministry and joined Web Industries in Atlanta, Georgia. Bob, on the other hand, is a born-again Christian who, as an entrepreneurial CEO, probably missed his real calling as a minister.

I remember so vividly our sense at that ESOP Conference that the ESOP Association needed a different direction and purpose. After some commiserating about the unknown leaders of the Association, we parted. Some weeks later, after the conference, I received a letter of invitation from Bob Fulton to attend a meeting at Web's corporate office in Westborough, Massachusetts, the purpose of which was to discuss the possible formation of the New England Chapter of the ESOP Association or a potential new local employee ownership organization to serve the New England states. That first and subsequent meetings of what was to be called the steering committee led to the formation of the New England Chapter of the ESOP Association with Bob Fulton as its first president and others of us serving in various chapter officer positions.

In the beginning it was not readily apparent to me where and how the work supporting this effort was being performed. Meeting agendas, written communications, mailings, phone communications, logistics, programming, etc. . . all done unselfishly, quietly, and well. Praise, recognition, and support were always abundantly distributed to others from Charles. This was all done in a manner that masked the efforts of the real contributor—Charles Edmunson.

Most of us have egos that sometimes interfere with growing and moving forward. We learned from Charles' absence of ego that imbuing any idea with its own respect and importance, regardless of whom or where the idea came from, was one catalyst for opening our minds to think more freely and creatively. Charles facilitated idea-generation so effortlessly and so subtly created a sense of high purpose that it called forth from each of us our best efforts. This quiet sense of purpose and absence of ego is at the heart of his ability to fathom the depths of each person's special talent and to gently over time free them to think and act beyond their own inner limits. The willing investment of his time and energy with the people he worked with always seemed to pay unexpected dividends. While some of us initially did not understand, Charles always knew those dividends would come. Charles' eleventh paradox ("With people, the shortest distance between two points is not a straight line.") applied to all of us who worked with him in the creation of the New England Chapter.

Because Charles is a gentle, patient, warm, understanding, disciplined, giving, forgiving, vulnerable, and empowering human being, he is by far the strongest person I have encountered in my 50-plus years in the adult world. Who among us could run each day for well over one thousand straight days with the seed of an unknown degenerative disease lurking in his body that progressively interfered with his physical functions. Charles' spirit is his driving force and the force that continues to this day to motivate those who interact with him.

In all the assignments and projects that Charles and I collaborated on over the last 10 years on behalf of the ESOP Association and employee ownership, there are memories of three experiences that continue to illuminate Charles' character and beliefs as a leader.

As good leaders instinctively know, leadership involves symbolic acts. Many in the ESOP community know the story of that one cold, snowy, and wet Sunday afternoon in Washington, D.C., after the completion of a four-hour session of the ESOP Association's first Strategic Planning Committee (preceded the evening before by a very-late-night working session for Charles and me at Charles' seemingly favorite working venue, Kinko's, drafting the ESOP Association's first vision statement). Although the values and beliefs embedded in the vision statement were clearly those of the Strategic Planning Committee and the leadership of the Association, they were in rough-draft form as pieces rather than as a coherent whole.

One of Charles' skills is his way of organizing thoughts, concepts, and words into a powerfully meaningful whole. When we finished in the wee hours of the morning, we both felt proud but somewhat anxious about the vision statement's acceptance by the Strategic Planning Committee. Would the committee recognize it as their own? . . . Truly it was . . . yet we wondered and worried.

At the completion of that Sunday morning meeting the Strategic Planning Committee gave unanimous support to the bold vision for a more equitable America that Charles and I had assembled. As we gathered our materials, Charles invited me to take a walk. He suggested that we walk to the Jefferson Memorial to let Thomas Jefferson listen to the ESOP Association's new vision for a better America. As we walked the two to three miles to the memorial through the snow, I vividly remember Charles talking of Jefferson's leadership, his contribution to our nation, and the potential for good inherent in the concept of employee ownership. When we reached the memorial, we both read aloud the vision statement with full confidence that if Tom were alive, he would approve of it.

Each year in May, at the ESOP Association's Annual Conference in Washington, D.C., we set off for the Jefferson Memorial to remind Tom that the desire for a better America is alive and well . . . and each year the number of our fellow employee owners who join us in this symbolic act grows. (In 1998 there were enough employee owners present for the National Park Rangers to inform us that we were now considered a demonstration . . . and of course, demonstrations are not permitted. We will continue to go each year but will probably have to read the vision statement silently.)

Leadership involves a commitment to care when those led are disheartened. During my last few years as an employee at Polaroid, there were times when either the commitment to support my ESOP Association activities was questioned or the value of this activity to the company would be at issue. Invariably during those times, Charles would either phone or be sitting in the lobby of the Polaroid plant where I worked, as I arrived in the morning. I marveled at his intuitiveness and timing—he always seemed to sense somehow the need I had at those times to be supported in the value of the work we were engaged in. He was always there to remind me, and it always made a difference.

Finally, in our work together I came fully to understand that the power of none of us is as smart as all of us, or as some would say, two heads are better than one. Charles talked of one plus one often equaling three, the product or synergy of two good thoughts or ideas leading to the emergence of a new, more creative and powerful idea. In my working relationship with Charles over the years, we both were able to say that each of us independently could do very good work but together could create something greater than the sum of our two parts. Charles facilitated the birth of those synergistic ideas because as a leader he was committed to the power of ideas to motivate. Isn't this an essential element of good leadership and business success?

According to Joseph Cambell, if you follow your bliss, you put yourself on a kind of track that has been there all the while, waiting for you, and the life that you ought to be living is the one you are living. Whatever you are in life, if you are following your bliss you are enjoying that refreshment, that spirit within you all the time. Until I met Charles I never understood what Cambell was writing about, particularly in regard to day-to-day organizational life.

Charles' belief that organizational life should nourish and sustain, should provide meaning and purpose for each of us is evident in his approach to the paradoxes of leadership. Leaders of the twenty-first century must see this as their overriding responsibility—as Edwin H. Land of Polaroid reminds us, the bottom line is in heaven.

On a personal note, Charles and I traveled extensively together on behalf of the ESOP Association and employee ownership. With a growing family, my wife would worry about me during any absence, except when she knew that Charles would be my traveling companion. She knew that Charles was always so calm, concerned, and caring that he would take care of anything that might go wrong. Although Charles is unable to travel with me anymore, he travels with me in spirit and in my heart. We love you Charles.

Reflections

DONNIE ROMINE

President of Web Industries

I have had the honor and privilege of sharing my working career with Charles Edmunson for 20 years. We have struggled together and learned together, sharing both success and disappointment along the journey, striving to build a special company. It is a delight to see Charles express so clearly that way of living and being that flows from who he is, from his very heart. He is a faithful practitioner of his beliefs, and he is my friend.

Anyone who meets Charles realizes very quickly that Charles is all about people. He is utterly committed to serving and to building others. I know of no one who is more fervent in their belief in the unique human potential of every individual. This undying belief in people and their potential is the fuel that propels his role as a nurturer. Charles never, ever, gives up on helping others become their best. For Charles, tasks, problems, or challenges, daunting as they may be, are simply new opportunities for helping people to learn, develop, and grow.

Being an effective nurturer, leader, and developer of others requires great skill. Charles is a person driven to excel, and he has worked diligently to learn for himself and then teach others. Even as Charles fights valiantly to rise above the disease that is slowly claiming his life, he is Charles, unselfishly and graciously teaching us about how to live and be effective for one another. Thank you, Charles: You always make us better!

Reflections

JUNE SEKERA

Corporation for Business, Work and Learning

I don't think a day goes by that I do not try to recall something Charles has taught me. Whether it is at work—in my interactions with people—or with friends, especially when I am unsure, or having difficulty, there is always something Charles has said to me, something that I can pull up from the recesses of my memory. And it helps.

I remember all sorts of things—from maxims to the lessons Charles has distilled for me from the many long and deep conversations we have shared.

One maxim that I often find useful is that none of us is as smart as all of us. Boy, does that cut through a lot of stuff. And when I say that in a meeting—particularly after there has been a successful struggle to find consensus—it not only helps me, but I think others understand its power.

Another is the quotation at the bottom of Bob Fulton's portrait: The most important thing in life is relationships. I'm still struggling with that one, trying to shoot from the hip less frequently than I'm constitutionally inclined to. Charles' life exemplified this maxim and has given so much help and hope to others simply by the way he related to them on an everyday basis.

The long conversations have had even more impact. How many times did I come to Charles when I was struggling? When I was trying to figure out how to deal with this problem or that? I don't know.

All I know is that when I went away after talking with Charles, I had a path to follow that I knew was the right one. I did not know if it would work, if it would get me where I wanted to be. That would depend on my execution of the plan. But I did know that if I did a good job on the execution, I would get to where I needed to be.

The problems that I brought to Charles usually had to do with how to relate to a person at work, most frequently with me as the boss. Charles helped me help each of those people grow. Left to my own devices, I would undoubtedly have not succeeded.

I can never thank Charles enough.

And I am still learning from him. Reading this book reminds me that his power to teach is unstoppable. Even this unjust disease does not prevent him from being the great leader that he is.

Even as the mechanics of his body fail to operate as he needs, his spirit crashes through and he keeps on helping and teaching. I feel his power every time the two of us talk, and every time I read from this book.

Charles, you are my teacher, my most important teacher. I am so fortunate and so privileged that my path crossed yours in this life. I love you dearly, not only for all that you have done for me, but also for the help you have given and the inspiration you have been for so many others in this life.

Reflections

SID SCOTT

Woodward Communications, Inc.

> *A paradox, a paradox, a most ingenious paradox . . .*
> —William S. Gilbert
> (from "The Pirates of Penzance," 1879)

When I read the insightful book by Charles Edmunson, many thoughts occurred. I would like to share some of those, hopefully to help as Charles has wished, to have this book change our lives. It is my feeling that no one else in the employee ownership community could have written such wise and yet so humble words.

I was reminded of my first meeting with Charles. The 1992 National Center for Employee Ownership annual conference, held in Chicago, was my initiation into the amazingly diverse world of employee ownership. As representatives from a new ESOP company (January of that year), Bill Skemp, our president, and I were attempting to learn as much as we could about our new retirement benefit/private ownership protection. What we discovered was that while we needed to understand the legal/technical aspects, we were missing an opportunity if we did not pursue the more complex opportunities to improve our company through communication and participation around broad ownership culture issues.

In order to get our money's worth from the conference, Bill and I attended separate sessions. One of the latter presentations featured two employee-owned companies, YSI and Web Industries. Corey Rosen served as the moderator. Following a very interesting overview of the YSI story by Malte vonMatthiesson, Charles was introduced. Although fatigued from information overload and having to sit for extended periods, something about Charles' demeanor was immediately intriguing, appealing, and energizing. Later, I was to understand that it was his genuine love of people and his uncommon honesty, which resonates throughout his book.

He particularly piqued my interest with his reflections on the purpose of a company. As an MBA graduate, like Charles, I had learned that the purpose of a company was to make a profit for (or maximize return to) the stockholders. In a very non-humanistic way, we were taught that employees, like capital, machinery, facilities, etc., were simply means (or tools) to that end. Charles, using values and broad ownership as catalysts, challenged us to think about the fact that employees, as stockholders in an employee-owned company, were both the means and ends. In other words, the purpose of our employee-owned company was to maximize the return to me as well as all of the other me's in the organization. Wow, I had experienced an epiphany! Educators call this type of situation a "teachable moment," when the learning variables present come together to help the student realize an important concept. A long time good friend and mentor of mine calls this experience an "Aha." Whatever we call it, the realization of this basic truth from Charles changed me forever. Hopefully, it has made me a better leader.

Through the years as we have made progress within our company, I have tapped the experiences of others, especially Web Industries. Charles has always been willing to share and encourage. Web's values (i.e., none of us is as smart as all of us, people are more important than profits) are broadly appealing and pragmatic. We owe much to him and the other lessons from the collective experiences of the ESOP community.

Charles reflected on Thomas Jefferson, the brilliant, talented, yet complex and human, revolutionary leader, whose life was a paradox in numerous ways. For many years, I have kept a copy of Jefferson's Rules of Living in my office. One rule, "Nothing is troublesome that we do willingly," is the essence for me of Charles' wisdom. If leaders understand people by listening, respect them for their humanness and individuality, and help them grow by allowing them to discover answers on their own, work will not be a burden, and we will all be better off. The paradoxes are that to do so means giving up our comfort with many of our concepts of what it means to be a successful leader.

Robert Browning said, "Ah, but a man's reach should exceed his grasp, or what's a heaven for?" For heaven's sake, what are we waiting for?

Tribute to Charles

JANET EDMUNSON

Wife
Product Manager, Blue Cross & Blue Shield of Massachusetts

Charles had been talking to me about his idea for a book for a number of years before he actually started writing it.

Unfortunately, Charles procrastinated and did not start writing this book until after his neurological disease started to overcome him. Before the book was finished, the disease had taken away Charles' ability to recollect some of his personal leadership experiences at Web that would have more strongly demonstrated the paradoxes.

Written tributes provided to Charles from employees and colleagues at Web, though, can help tell these stories. They demonstrate how beautifully Charles put into practice the paradoxes that he has shared with you in this book. Charles is truly a unique and special leader who cared first and foremost about the employees at Web.

I would like to share some thoughts from his friends and co-workers. These excerpts confirm Charles' practical application of the paradoxes that ruled his life.

~

Charles has a special "people oriented" quality. . . . Charles conveys to me a sense of being listened to, appreciated, and valued. I frequently come away from spending time with Charles feeling more confident and excited about the future for both myself and the company.

Wayne Potter
Sales Manager, Web Converting of Indianapolis

You have enlightened me to challenge myself and issues that arise from conflict.

Jeannine Gilmore
Former Administrative Assistant, Web Industries Corporate Office

Charles is our Vice President of Manufacturing, but his title should be "Vice President of Interpersonal Relationships." . . . Although his knowledge of converting got him to his present position, it is his love for his fellow workers that will be his legacy. . . . By his actions, Charles reminds me that people always come first!

Bev Radloff
Quality Management Representative, Web Converting of Indianapolis

I am different because of Charles. His constant and unwavering respect and sensitivity for each individual's value is an enduring example. I often joke, in front of Charles, that most of my sensitivity I got from Charles.

Donnie Romine
President, Web Industries

Charles has not only encouraged and supported me, but he has challenged me also. . . . It's important for all of us in our lives to know that there is someone who will listen and care, and I feel lucky to be working with Charles and people like him.

David M. Turner
Director of Training & Logistics, Web Converting of Framingham

Your special gift to me has always been in the way you look at me and see the person I want to be. . . . Whenever you are near, I get a transfusion of confidence and self esteem. . . . I know you truly believe that human nature makes every person want to be the best person they can be. The amazing thing is you can communicate that faith in me.

Sharon Morin
Administrative Assistant, Web Industries Corporate Office

Charles is a better editor than I am and I never felt put down by any of his corrections—and you know what big egos writers have! . . . I felt entirely like I was going to succeed because of Charles' help.

Bob Waggoner
General Manager, Web Converting of Dallas

Charles means a lot to me. Charles helped me. . . . Charles encourages people and supports them.

Pao Her
Machine Operator, Web Converting of Atlanta

He cares a lot about people working on the floor especially. . . . People loved to work for him.

Pheng Rattanong
Machine Operator, Web Converting of Atlanta

When I asked for some time to chat, he basically dropped everything. There were many beneficial pieces of wisdom he imparted, but none greater than making me feel valued.

Chris Boone

Sales Manager, Web Converting of Indianapolis

Charles is a very good listener. That I know very well.

Lloyd Roberts

Machine Operator, Web Converting of Atlanta

Perhaps the thing that Charles teaches me the most is in his ability to "give grace" to others. I can't think of anyone else that I know whose reflexive response with people is to give them grace—in the form of immediate openness, acceptance, valuing them as people, forgiveness, caring, or whatever other form that may take.

Dan Ott

Vice President of Sales, Web Industries

Charles is a good guy. He took time to talk to each person. . . . I respect him like a brother.

Bo Luangsombath

Machine Operator, Web Converting of Atlanta

Charles takes care of the employee first. . . . I love to work with Charles. He's a good team player.

Baldev Patel

Machine Operator, Web Converting of Atlanta

Charles has taught me so much about how to get to people's hearts, how to treat them with respect, and do for them what he has done for me.

Lauren Richardson

Director Total Quality Ownership Education, Web Industries

Charles gives me the initiative to do things I don't think are possible. Things that I think are out of my grasp, he shows me are in my grasp.

Joshua McLaughlin

Machine Operator, Web Converting of Atlanta

The most important things I believe Charles has shared with me: how, as leaders, the daily impact our behavior has on our co-workers; the importance of being a good listener; caring about people; and leading by example.

Norm Gould

Production Manager, Web Converting of Indianapolis

There are times when I doubt the power of people and their potential. . . . It is at these times that I feel the energy of your commitment to the potential of people. I lose my doubts.

Hugh McGill
Director of Organizational Development & Quality, Web Converting of Framingham

Charles is the best teacher by example of the inherent worth of people that I've ever had.

Michelle Quinn
Sales Coordinator & Senior Account Manager, Web Converting of Framingham

I knew that what made you different is that you give people a chance to rise to their potential.

Shirsten Dreyer
Editor of The Web Guide, *Web Industries*

The example you set by your hard work, enthusiasm, and encouragement of others helped build a strong foundation for the plant.

John Duncan
Converting Solutions Specialist, Web Industries

Charles would always find the time for others. Even though his schedule would be full he would make the time to listen.

Rich Scali
Formerly of Web Converting of Framingham

It was easy to be open or "transparent" with Charles because the only criticism he ever had for you was constructive. He wanted me to learn from my mistakes, and not dwell on them.

Charlie Belcher
Sales Manager, Film X Products

The first thing that comes to mind (when I think of Charles) is the thought that there are not many people I have met who care for people more than Charles does. . . . The guy is like a big heart with legs.

Carl Rubin
Vice President of Finance, Web Industries

He has been genuine, honest, and always supportive and without his encouragement and support I know my job would have been more difficult and much less fun.

Karl Kussro
General Manager, Web Converting of Indianapolis

He is the type of person who always looks for the positive in people and would do whatever is necessary to bring the positive out of the people he is associated with.

Al Koles
Formerly of Web Converting of Atlanta

Appendices

Charles' Disease–PSP

In the early stages, one doctor simply called it "Charles' Disease." After three years, doctors finally began to suspect it was in fact PSP—progressive supranuclear palsy.

It started insidiously when Charles was 46 years old. While shooting a video, he noticed that he was having trouble keeping up with the others as they ran up the stairs of the Jefferson Memorial in Washington, D.C. He also had some difficulty with his eye-hand coordination when taking change from a cashier. As the disease progressed and he continued to lose depth perception, stairs became even more difficult, driving became treacherous, and reading was impossible because his eyes couldn't track across the line. PSP attacked his eyes—and finally rendered him legally blind.

PSP usually occurs in older people. But doctors are seeing it increasingly in people in their forties. In just four years since his first symptoms, Charles suffered significant losses in his physical abilities. PSP has taken away Charles' ability to walk and run, but not without Charles giving it a good fight. He succeeded in running over 1,400 days in a row (starting before he noticed the disease). Charles tried to keep that streak going as long as he could—even by using shopping carts at the grocery store for support as he circled the parking lot with his wife's support.

PSP has also stolen Charles' ability to speak. This has been the most difficult result of the disease for Charles. He is an exceptionally bright man, full of ideas—a talented public speaker and communicator. Charles needs total care for his daily needs now. Someone—home health aides, his wife, and other family members and friends—are with him each hour of the day.

Charles has always led a mission-focused life to make a difference in the world by caring for others. He never lost that vision, even with the assault of this disease on his body. PSP is winning the battle for the body. But it will never conquer his spirit.

Editor's Note: Charles' autopsy report showed that Charles had a related disease to PSP called corticobasal degeneration (CBD). This would not have changed any of his treatments.

Facts About PSP and CBD
(Progressive Supranuclear Palsy and Corticobasal Degeneration)

What Are PSP and CBD?

Progressive supranuclear palsy (PSP) and corticobasal degeneration (CBD) are neurodegenerative brain diseases that have no known cause, treatment or cure. They affect nerve cells that control walking, balance, mobility, vision, speech, and swallowing. Five to six people per 100,000 will develop PSP. That ratio is even smaller for CBD patients. Symptoms begin, on average, when an individual is in the early 60's, but may start as early as in the 40's. PSP is slightly more common in men than women, but PSP has no known geographical, occupational or racial preference.

PSP displays a wide range of symptoms including:

- Loss of balance.
- Changes in personality such as a loss of interest in ordinary pleasurable activities or increased irritability.
- Weakness of eye movements, especially in the downward direction.
- Weakened movements of the mouth, tongue and throat.
- Slurred speech.
- Difficulty swallowing.

Symptoms of CBD include:

- Stiffness, shakiness, jerkiness, slowness, and clumsiness in either the upper or lower extremities
- Difficulty with speech generation (dysphasia)
- Difficulty with articulation (dysarthria)

- Difficulty controlling the muscles of the face and mouth
- Walking and balance difficulty
- Asymmetric onset of symptoms (occuring on one side of the body first then gradually moving to the other side)
- Memory or behavior problems

How Are PSP and CBD Diagnosed?

PSP and CBD are usually diagnosed by a neurologist. There is no diagnostic test other than the clinical evaluation. Typical findings include features of Parkinson's with limb stiffness, slowness, imbalance, and trouble walking with limitation of upward and downward eye movements (especially with PSP).

Can People Die from PSP or CBD?

Yes. People with PSP or CBD die from complications of immobility and the inability to swallow, including pneumonia and aspiration.

What Is the Treatment?

PSP and CBD currently have no direct course of effective treatment or medication, although some drugs and therapies provide temporary or modest benefit to treat symptoms.

What Is the Foundation for PSP / CBD and Related Brain Diseases (Foundation)?

The Foundation is a nonprofit 501(c)3 charitable organization that is governed by a national board of directors and an internationally renowned medical advisory board. All donations support the organization, educational efforts and medical research.

How Can the Foundation Help?

As a worldwide organization, the Foundation sponsors medical research and provides information, education, support, and advocacy to persons with PSP and CBD, their families, and caregivers. The Foundation educates physicians and allied health professionals on PSP and CBD and how to improve care.

For more information or to make a contribution, contact:

Foundation for PSP / CBD and Related Brain Diseases
11350 McCormick Road, Executive Plaza III, Suite 906
Hunt Valley, MD 21031
Phone: 1-800-457-4777
Fax: 410-785-7009
Website: http://www.psp.org

Order Form for *Paradoxes of Leadership*

Paradoxes of Leadership is published by the National Center for Employee Ownership (NCEO). It costs $15 per copy, plus shipping (and sales tax for California residents). You can order additional copies online at our Web site (**www.nceo.org**)*;* by telephoning the NCEO at 510-208-1300; or by mailing or faxing a copy of this form.

Name

Organization

Address

City, State, Zip (Country)

Telephone   Fax   Email

Method of Payment: ❑ Check (payable to "NCEO")   ❑ Visa   ❑ M/C   ❑ AMEX

Credit Card Number

Signature   Exp. Date

Checks are accepted only for orders from the U.S. and must be in U.S. currency.

Quantity of *Paradoxes of Leadership* @ $15 each _____	**Subtotal** _____	$
Sales Tax: California residents add 8.75% sales tax	**Sales Tax** _____	$
Shipping: In the U.S., first book $5, each additional book $1; elsewhere, we charge exact shipping costs to your credit card, plus a $10 handling surcharge	**Shipping** _____	$
	TOTAL DUE _____	$

Fax (credit card orders only) to 510-272-9510

Mail (credit card or check orders) to:

NCEO
1736 Franklin Street, 8th Floor
Oakland, CA 94612